IMAGES OF ENGLAND

AROUND
HASLEMERE

The view looking north from the town hall on the occasion of a meet of the Chiddingfold Hunt during the winter of 1912. This Hunt used to meet regularly outside the Kings Arms, an indication of just how close open countryside and farmland was to the High Street. In the foreground the new electricity sub-station built in 1911 provided power for a multi-branch electric street light. However, the gaslights first installed around 1870 continued to light the street until much later. The group of tile-hung shops in the background were demolished in the summer of 1912 and replaced by the London County & Westminster Bank, a building now occupied by the Natwest Bank Ltd.

IMAGES OF ENGLAND

AROUND HASLEMERE

TIM WINTER

First published in 2002 by Tempus Publishing

Reprinted in 2010 by
The History Press
The Mill, Brimscombe Port,
Stroud, Gloucestershire, GL5 2QG
www.thehistorypress.co.uk

Copyright © Tim Winter, 2010

ISBN 978 0 7524 2481 1

Typesetting and origination by
Tempus Publishing Limited
Printed and bound in Great Britain by
Marston Book Services Limited, Didcot

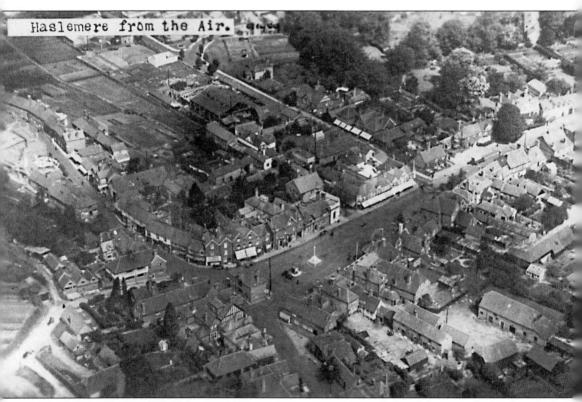

Haslemere from the Air.

An aerial view of Haslemere in 1922, an opportunity to view 'behind the scenes' in and around the High Street. Many of the buildings fronting the road remain unchanged today, but stables and other outbuildings behind have changed, or disappeared altogether. The development of West Street was still not completed and the line of trees in Chestnut Avenue continued around the corner to where the police station was soon to be built. The large area between Lower Street and West Street, once known as Bunkhurst Meadows, was covered in various crops growing in small patches or allotments. As early as 1820 this land had been offered at auction with outline plans for housing, a development that never took place allowing car parking and other commercial uses to flourish during the twentieth century.

Contents

Three young girls picking blackberries around 1904 in Scotlands Lane.

Acknowledgements

The compilation of this book would not have been possible without the help of many friends and relatives. I am also very grateful to the many photographers, some named but others unknown, who took the pictures I have used. A special thank you to the Haslemere Educational Museum for allowing me access to the photographic collection in their archives. The following people and institutions gave permission to use their pictures or helped in the preparation of this book:

Aldershot & District Bus Interest Group, Donald Birkenshaw, Graham Collyer, Mrs S.J. Day, the late Colin Futcher, Joy Glover, Geoffrey Godden, John Goodrum, Grayswood School, Martin Green, Peter Hall, Haslemere Education Museum, the *Haslemere Herald*, Rick Ingrams, Dr Peter Lane, R. and G. Madgwick, Peter Moorey, The National Trust, Mrs M.E.M. Oldreive, Lee Peck, Richard Peskett, Vi and Cyril Queen, Mrs Riddle, Brian Silver, the *Surrey Advertiser*, Transco National Gas Archive, Greta Turner, Tony Waddell, Peter Waller, Waverley Borough Council, John White, Ruby Winter, Tony Wright.

Among the books, local guides and pamphlets consulted the following were very useful sources:

Hindhead or The English Switzerland, 2nd Edition, Thomas Wright (1907); *Bygone Haslemere*, E.W. Stanton (1924); *Haslemere in History*, G.R. Rolston (1956); *Haslemere 1850-1950*, G.R. Rolston (1964); *Grayshott*, J.H. Smith (1978); *Around Haslemere and Hindhead in old photographs*, Tim Winter & Graham Collyer (1991); *A Country Museum Revisited*, Martin Kane (1995); *The Post of Haslemere*, Peter Moorey (1998); *Fifty Years of the West Sussex Fire Brigade 1948-1998*, S. Jordan (1999); *The Flowers that Bloomed in the Spring*, Fay Foster (no date); *The Lost Arts of Europe* The Haslemere Museum Collection of European Peasant Art, David Crowley and Lou Taylor ed. (2000).

Finally a special thank you to my wife Jackie for her tolerance and help during the preparation of this book.

Introduction

The position of Haslemere in the extreme south-west corner of Surrey where three counties meet, means that any account of the area will also include places in Hampshire and West Sussex. The town is situated in the deep, clay-bottomed valleys cut by tributary streams of the River Wey through hills formed from the Lower Greensand rocks around Hindhead, Marley and Blackdown. Large parts of these sandy heights are covered by open heathland and woodland, much of which is now owned and managed by The National Trust. Indeed, the primary reason for the formation of the Trust in 1895 was to protect these areas of great natural beauty from over-development. Sir Robert Hunter, who was solicitor to the General Post Office and lived in Three Gates Lane, Haslemere, was a founder member of the small group whose actions included the protection of footpath rights and saving several important areas of heathland around Hindhead and Grayshott. These original sites formed a focus around which large areas are now free from any future development and open for all to enjoy.

Much of the threat to the heathlands followed the opening of the London to Portsmouth railway line in 1859. Until then Haslemere had not been on any important route through southern England and the town stayed quite small. The main coach road to Portsmouth passed over Hindhead and, although horse-drawn coaches struggling across the heavy clay soils between Guildford and Chichester passed through Haslemere, this was not a route which brought much trade or prosperity to the town. But, once a convenient rail link to London was established, the benefits of living on the dry and airy hills around Haslemere and Hindhead made this an ideal environment for many more affluent people to live far from the pollution in large towns and cities. Two of the first people to discover these benefits were Alfred Lord Tennyson, who built his summer home on Blackdown, and the scientist Professor John Tyndall, whose love of mountains brought him to Hindhead, which he said reminded him of Switzerland, and where in the 1880s he built Hindhead House, just south of the crossroads. Soon afterwards several writers came to live in or near Hindhead – including George Bernard Shaw, Grant Allen, the poet Richard Le Gallienne who lived at Moorlands, and Sir Arthur Conan Doyle. Earlier in the nineteenth century another famous poet, Christina Rosetti, whose brother was the artist Dante Gabriel Rosetti, came to live in Shottermill at Brookbank, the house where George Eliot lived soon afterwards (see p. 104). Even earlier in 1838 the wild scenery of the Devil's Punch Bowl had been described by Charles Dickens in *Nicholas Nickleby* when Smike and Nicholas travelled along the London to Portsmouth road. Later, this same scenery, and the infamous murder of a sailor here in 1786, inspired the Revd Baring Gould to write his novel *The Broom Squire*.

Many artists were attracted to live in the area around Haslemere towards the end of the nineteenth century, including Josiah Wood Whymper, Walter Tyndale, W. Biscombe Gardner and the sculptor Albert Bruce-Joy. A group of artists lived in nearby Witley including Myles Burkett Foster and Helen Allingham. The later visited Haslemere a number of times and painted local scenes at Shottermill and Shepherds Hill as well as Mr Williamson's fish shop in the High Street.

The good rail link to London and the coast helped attract wealthy business people and others including the book publishers Alexander Macmillan and Sir Algenon Methuen, the Brooklands motor ace Selwyn Francis Edge, Lord Aberconwy and the Hon. Rollo Russell, who all built large houses around Hindhead. All this in spite of William Cobbett having described the Devil's Punch Bowl as 'the most villainous spot that God ever made' in his *Rural Rides* published just over half a century earlier.

The period of expansion around Haslemere from the 1890s into the early twentieth century coincided with the development and spread of the peasant art movement in Britain. In Haslemere the arrival of Joseph and Maud King in 1894, followed two years later by Godfrey Blount and his wife Ethel, who was Maud King's sister, marked the beginning of peasant arts in Haslemere. The Kings founded The Wheel and Spinners Guild, which became the Haslemere Weaving Industry in 1897 (see p. 49). Godfrey Blount had trained as a designer and was chairman of the English Handicraft Society. In Haslemere his designs were used on the silk weaving looms established by Edmund Hunter at St Edmundsbury. From 1902 the Blount's lived in Weydown Road where they established the St Cross School of Handicraft. Another silk weaving house was opened by Harry Hedges at Spitalfields, a small wooden building close to the stream at the bottom of Wey Hill. Other craftsmen attracted to the area by the growth of the newly formed Peasant Arts Society included Romney Green who manufactured furniture in Kings Road, William Stallworthy and Radley Young who established an art pottery at Hammer (see p. 73) and the bookbinder Miss Hay Cooper. An exhibition of craft work held in Haslemere School in 1905 included woven silk, woollen rugs and carpets, furniture and wrought iron work. It was attended by Her Majesty Queen Alexandra who made several purchases and ordered other items to be made by local craftsmen.

After the First World War the craft industries in Haslemere and elsewhere declined and the Peasant Arts Society, which had been founded by Joseph King, finished in 1933. Very few photographic images of this important period in the life of the town seem to have survived. However, many of the artefacts, originally collected by members of the Peasant Arts Society and kept in their museum at No. 1 The Pavement in Haslemere High Street, and later at Foundry Meadows in Kings Road, are now in the Haslemere Educational Museum where the collection was moved in 1926 under the care of Joseph King.

For much of the photographic record of this area we are in debt to the postcard photographers and publishers who, by chance, documented many of the changes that took place in and around the town at the beginning of the twentieth century. Picture postcards were first allowed by the Post Office in Britain from September 1894. Soon after 1900 national publishers such as Francis Frith, Fred Judge and James Valentine were producing many different view cards. They were quickly followed by local shops and photographers who published their own postcards, the most prolific being Haslemere pharmacist Edward Gane Inge who issued several hundred different local views on cards during the Edwardian era. Large numbers of these postcards were bought by visitors to the area and have left an accessible and enduring record of life in and around the town during the first half of the twentieth century.

I do hope that you, the reader, will have as much enjoyment from the collection of images in this book as I have had in bringing them together.

Tim Winter,
February 2002.
Revised October 2010

One

Haslemere

The High Street looking north in the late 1880s, just before the seventeenth-century Swan Inn was rebuilt. Just past the inn a man is bending over the horse trough given by Mr James Stewart Hodgson, a wealthy landowner who lived at Lythe Hill House, to mark the Golden Jubilee of Queen Victoria in 1887. Across the road many of the shops and houses were to be changed or demolished during the next forty years. The shop to the right was a butchers run by Alfred Softley. Next door were the premises of T. Hack and the triple-gabled front of Stephen Tanner's shop. Three of the town's inhabitants are listed under the original photograph as 'The Haslemere Drunkard [about to enter the Swan], the Band of Hope Boy [centre] and the British Woman', an amusing comment by Mrs Newman, a contemporary local resident.

The original photograph of this view dates from around 1880 but was published as a postcard in 1901 when there was still a very intimate relationship between the town of Haslemere and the surrounding farmland. North-west of the High Street fields spread towards the hills of Hindhead which were then covered mainly in heathland and not so thickly wooded as today. The cattle in the foreground were grazing in fields that formed part of Half Moon Farm; the farmhouse and other buildings were situated in East Street or Petworth Road, just opposite the town hall.

By around 1885 the old ivy-covered shop that stood on the corner of Shepherds Hill and Lower Street was already looking very dilapidated. It was demolished in the early 1900s but the site remained empty until about fifteen years ago when two new shops were built further back. The building next door, that still makes this corner very narrow, was a bank at the end of the nineteenth century. In 1909 Richard Harrison opened a pharmacy here; he already owned the pharmacy in Grayshott which he had bought from his former employer, Edward Gane Inge. When Mr Inge moved to Norfolk in 1909 he sold his shops in Haslemere and Chiddingfold to Messrs Wiles and Holman. He was known to have been annoyed to hear that his former employee had opened in competition with Wiles and Holman – not the correct thing to do at that time.

The deserted High Street, looking north on an afternoon in around 1870, was still largely unaffected by the arrival of the railway in the town a few years before, despite the great influence this was to have during the next century. Beyond the old Swan Inn on the left are a shop and cottages that were replaced in 1886 by the Workman's Institute, now the Comrades Club, the very generous gift of Mr Stewart Hodgson. In the distance the crown of the old horse chestnut tree, reputedly planted in 1792, appears almost as large as it is today.

Shops on the corner opposite the town hall around 1904 included a butcher and the grocery shop of Otways, who also had shops in Petworth. The delivery cart on the left belongs to another grocer, Charles Burgess, whose Broadway Stores were on the corner of West Street. Mr Burgess also had shops at Hindhead, Liphook and Lion Green (now Bells Stores).

Shops along the east side of the High Street during the 1890s included Alf Softley, butcher, between Enticknap's boot shop and the White Horse, and Mrs Bridger, an insurance agent, in premises now occupied by Keats Harding. Outside the White Horse there is a penny farthing bicycle and a tricycle. Perhaps the riders were just enjoying Haslemere hospitality at the inn? Or maybe these were new machines – there was a bicycle maker in the High Street, F. Knibb, whose cycle depot also sold and hired all leading makes of machines at this time.

The last fair to be held in the High Street was in 1904. The Charter granted by Queen Elizabeth I in 1596 authorized the holding of a market every Tuesday and two annual fairs, one on the Feast of Saint Philip and Saint James, the other on the eve of the Feast of the Rising of the Cross. In 1906 the fairs moved to Wey Hill (see p. 90) after one year in Town Meadow.

The present town hall was built in 1814. The arches at the bottom, now filled by windows, were opened originally to the ground with the space between enclosed by metal railings. There was an infants' school in the room upstairs until 1900. The Aldershot and District Traction Company buses from Farnham terminated outside the town hall from 1913 until the bus bay was constructed in Lower Street. The public house behind the bus was the Kings Arms and William Dea's grocery shop was on the left of the Petworth Road.

The Kings Arms stood next to the White Horse Hotel on the east side of the High Street. A Foden the steam lorry from Friary, Holroyd & Healy's Brewery at Guildford was delivering Friary Ales in around 1909 to the Kings Arms. It was outside this public house in 1855 that a gang of navvies, employed to build the new railway line from Farncombe to Havant, were involved in a drunken brawl that led to the death of Police Inspector William Donaldson. Although it was never discovered who struck the fatal blow with an iron bar, four of the five men sent for trial were found guilt of manslaughter. The ringleader, Thomas Wood, was transported to Australia for twenty years.

Swan Hotel,

THE RIVIERA OF ENGLAND.

600 ft. above sea level.
7 minutes from Station.

Haslemere, Surrey.

Stabling and Good Accommodation for Motors.

E. HODGES, *Proprietor.*

After extensive rebuilding in the 1890s the Swan Inn became known as the Swan Hotel, evidently hoping to attract some of the increasing number of visitors coming to the area. This advertising leaflet dates from around 1905 and lists the many attractions offered by Mr Hodges, although comparison of the local climate with that of the Mediterranean was perhaps rather exaggerated!

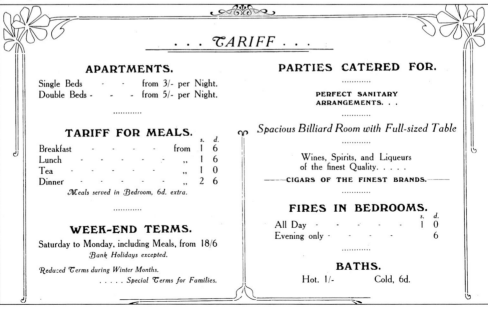

. . . TARIFF . . .

APARTMENTS.

Single Beds	from 3/- per Night.
Double Beds	from 5/- per Night.

TARIFF FOR MEALS.

		s.	d.
Breakfast	from	1	6
Lunch	,,	1	6
Tea	,,	1	0
Dinner	,,	2	6

Meals served in Bedroom, 6d. extra.

WEEK-END TERMS.

Saturday to Monday, including Meals, from 18/6
Bank Holidays excepted.

Reduced Terms during Winter Months.
. . . . . *Special Terms for Families.*

PARTIES CATERED FOR.

PERFECT SANITARY ARRANGEMENTS. . .

Spacious Billiard Room with Full-sized Table

Wines, Spirits, and Liqueurs of the finest Quality. . . . .
———CIGARS OF THE FINEST BRANDS.———

FIRES IN BEDROOMS.

	s.	d.
All Day	1	0
Evening only		6

BATHS.

Hot. 1/-   Cold, 6d.

What a difference a century makes! This quiet weekday scene dates from around 1903. A cart laden with the baggage of visitors to the Swan Hotel stands by the horse trough outside the Haslemere Institute. Across the road another horse waits patiently outside the pharmacy of Edward Gane Inge, who also published many interesting postcards of the area during the early 1900s. He also had shops in Grayshott, Bordon, Liphook and Chiddingfold. Although he was in business here for only about ten years he and his wife played an active part in the town, being on various committees including the Church of England Men's Society and the Mothers' Union. He was a sidesman at St Bartholomew's church, a member of the Church Council in 1907, secretary of the Haslemere Rifle Club and even found time to serve in the Surrey Volunteer Brigade with the rank of sergeant.

The large banner hanging outside the Capital and Counties Bank (now Lloyds) is asking people to buy War Bonds. Considerable sums of money were raised from the public in this way during the First World War. Posters in the shop windows advertise War Savings Certificates and a War Weapons Week – a campaign we never wish to see again.

The White Horse was a thriving inn in Victorian times as shown in this *carte de visite* photograph of about 1860. It had been described as a 'commercial inn' in Pigots' Directory of 1842 when the landlord was William Harrison. During the eighteenth century the Haslemere postmaster was at the White Horse from where mail was dispatched by coach or rider. The *Duke of Richmond* coach from London to Chichester called here daily at half past eleven every morning. The returning coach stopped at two o'clock in the afternoon. After the railway was built to Woking the coaches were transferred to a train for the final leg of their journey to London.

Post-war Britain and the High Street in 1947 is looking much the same as today apart from the cars parked in the centre of the road. Next to the War Memorial, designed by local architect Inigo Triggs, is a van belonging to Bertram Mills Circus – perhaps they were performing at the Wey Hill fairground.

Soon after the arrival of the motor car came motor engineers and petrol stations. Green and Co. were the first in the High Street, having moved from their original premises in Lower Street. The proprietor, centre left wearing a cap, was Walter Smithers Green. The hand-cranked petrol pump, maybe the first in the town, was being used around 1922 to fill the tank of a chauffeur-driven car with Pratt's Perfection motor spirit. After the garage closed in 1968 the re-built premises were occupied by Boots the Chemist who had moved across the road from Causewayside.

By 1910 W.J. Mercer had succeeded Mr Furlonger at the butcher's shop opposite West Street and the usual Edwardian period display of meat hung outside for inspection by the flies as well as by his customers. Later the shop became Elphicks but, after the business was bought about sixty years ago by W. Pink & Sons, the old shop and house were replaced with the present building in 1939; groceries, wines and spirits were sold from the new and much larger shop.

The west side of the High Street in the 1880s. The large house on the extreme left, the home of Dr Henry Clothier, was demolished in the 1890s and replaced by The Broadway, the block of shops still there today. The gap by the lamp-post is where West Street was built in 1899 to give access to the new school in Chestnut Avenue. The building with the very tall chimney was once the Angel Inn, a name still remembered as the mid-1920s re-development of this corner is called Angel Buildings. The cottages at Causewayside became shops from about 1900. The last one before the old chestnut tree had a dormer window added at about this time and became a florist's shop run by A. Evans.

The opposite side of the High Street in the 1880s and W. Furlonger had the blind shut at his butcher's shop. Next door was the house of Dr Whiting, the local medical officer of health in the early 1900s. This is now two shops but the cottages next door were pulled down when a new garage and car showrooms were built there by the Haslemere Motor Company. Their first garage had been in Lower Street, opposite the bottom of Shepherds Hill – a building now used for the sale of beds. The two men with a cart were repairing potholes in the road using chert rock that had been quarried locally. The main roads were not surfaced with tarmacadam until thirty years later.

The upper part of the High Street around 1905 appears very similar to today. The shop that was the square bay window of the Small House, behind the posts and chains (see next page) had become a private house. The next building was once called Goodwyns. It was here that John Morley the surveyor was living when he first drew a plan of Haslemere Borough in about 1722. His second map in 1735 showed clear details of the buildings around the High Street and listed the freeholders of each property. Further down the street were the three pollarded trees that later gave their name to the Three Limes Tea Rooms. On the corner of Well Lane there was a large advertising sign for the West Sussex Gazette and for the manufacture and repair of umbrellas, presumably at one of the three new shops built in 1897 next to Well Lane.

This little shop was at the north end of the lovely old house hung with fish-scale tiles next to Well Lane. During the early part of the twentieth century it had been a favourite place for children when it was a sweet shop. By the time this postcard was published in the late 1930s (note the air-raid precaution tape across the windows to stop the glass shattering) it was the showroom of Haslemere Weaving and Handicrafts. The proprietor was E. Hosslin and the workrooms where cotton and linen goods were made, known as the Weaving House, were at Tythe Patch behind the post office. More recently this building was used by both the Haslemere Players and the Thespians for rehearsals and scenery work, but was partially destroyed by fire in August 1997.

Town House at the northern end of the High Street in about 1880. It was built in the orchard of the old farmhouse known as Quennells. In the early eighteenth century John Tanner and his son, both lawyers, lived there, but in 1747 it was sold to General James Oglethorpe. He had been elected as one of Haslemere's MPs in 1722 but is better known for founding the colony of Georgia in America some ten years later. However, he had a house called Westbrook at Godalming and probably never lived in Haslemere. From 1768 the infamous Revd James Fielding, curate of Haslemere, lived in Town House with his wife and family. He is believed to have been involved in robbing mail coaches during the time he lived there, and later some mail bags were found in the cellars. During the latter part of the Victorian era artist J.W. Whymper lived in the house. His son Edward, also an artist, was the first mountaineer to climb the Matterhorn in 1865. The little shop on the right had closed by the beginning of the twentieth century.

Pictured around 1910 this large white house was called The Lodge and was the home of Miss Hesse. Her father, the Revd Hesse, had been the last rector of Chiddingfold parish when it still included much of Haslemere. When she died her nephew, Major John Hesse, moved across the road to Olivers and, in 1926, The Lodge became the new home for the Haslemere Educational Museum. The large doors on the left may have originally given access for carriages. The far part of the building with no windows used to be the laundry but is now Museum Cottage.

Two

More Haslemere

The Old Malt House in Lower Street, with the attached corn merchants shop at the corner of Shepherds Hill, made the roadway in 1880 very narrow indeed. Although the population of Haslemere was beginning to increase it was still under 2,000 and the need for a better road was still in the future. Major widening did not take place here until the late 1930s when all the buildings in the foreground were demolished. During the Second World War this area was the site for an underground air-raid shelter but was grassed over and the stone walls, seats and a bus bay made some fifty years ago.

The view along Lower Street towards the railway station in 1908 also shows how narrow this road used to be. The single-storey shop with the sun blinds down was T. Oldershaw, Colonial Butcher, until the First World War. In the early 1920s another local man, Gilbert King, opened the Covent Garden Fruit and Vegetable Store here. The low wall and decorative iron railings disappeared when the road was widened.

In 1910 there were quite a few small shops along the High Pavement in Lower Street. On the left was W.C. Waterston's Stores selling groceries, provisions and freshly baked bread. A large tea cannister hanging above the shop advertises the 'Golden Tea House' where the writer of this postcard has just had tea. Beyond the shops is the Good Intent inn. Across the road and almost hidden was the forge of Mr William Maides, maker of much fine wrought ironwork including the gates to Haslemere School (see p. 26) and those at the Manor House in Three Gates Lane. The latter were designed by Professor G. Aitchinson RA in the Renaissance style for Lythe Hill House but were installed instead at the Manor House after the death of Mr Hodgson in 1899. They were moved to Ireland when his son-in-law became Marquis of Sligo. Apparently the replacement gates were saved from being scrapped during the Second World War by being sunk in the garden pond.

Mr W. Fagent ran his plumbing and decorating business from this three-storey Georgian house on the north side of Lower Street. A fine show of roses on the wall and the wearing of straw boaters suggest it was a summer's day during the First World War. Local trade directories show the address as Station Road in 1900, but Lower Street by 1905; before the railway came it was called Pilewell or Pylewell Street as it led to the well of that name. The cottage to the right and the shop to the left, once Stone's China Shop, have both been demolished since the Second World War.

This pair of tile-hung Victorian houses known as The Gables dominate the view along the High Pavement in Lower Street, c. 1885. During the 1930s the left-hand house was a shop run by W. Hall who sold newspapers, tobacco, sweets and sheet music. Mr and Mrs Raggett continued the newsagent's business at The Gables from 1959 until 1978 when it became a private house. Next door the bowler-hatted carpenter was working outside the Good Intent, opened in 1867 by a Godalming brewer but closed before 1939. The closest house on the left was demolished in the 1960s. Further along the terrace of cottages next to the Baptist chapel had only just been built when John Wornham Penfold recorded this view.

The Pylewell, or Pilewell, was one of the two wells used for the public water supply in Haslemere and was just below the cottage on the left. After it became polluted a new well was sunk on the bank opposite. From here a piped water supply was started in about 1890 by Mr James Stewart Hodgson. Water was pumped from the new well to a storage tank on Shepherds Hill. This head of water ensured adequate pressure in the town's taps. Water pressure was not a problem after two new reservoirs were built on Blackdown in 1907 and a well sunk to 137 feet (42 metres). These reservoirs held 111,000 gallons (504,000 litres) and 400,000 gallons (1.8 million litres) respectively.

Looking across towards Lower Street from above Sandrock, c. 1910. The lorry passing Glen Cottage belonged to William Godfrey Ltd of Haslemere and Hindhead. Further up the hill was the stonemason's yard where many of the tombstones in local churchyards were carved. Next door was Ye Olde Curiosity Shoppe where Mr Brunel Hoyes sold antique furniture and also carried out repairs, polishing and upholstery. Opposite his shop the new Congregational church had been built in 1880-81 adjoining an earlier chapel built in 1804. The old chapel had been lit by gas since 1869. The Revd Charles Morgan, pastor from 1839 to 1872, took an active part in the introduction of this new form of lighting after the gas works opened in 1868 (see p. 84)

Soon after 1900 the view from Shepherds Hill showed a predominantly rural landscape to the west of the town centre. In the large glasshouses to the left tomatoes, strawberries and flowers were grown at Oaklands Nursery (see p. 28). The new Haslemere School at the top of Chestnut Avenue, centre right, had just been built, marking the beginning of the westward spread of the town. The back of the Congregational church, recently converted into homes, and the cottages at Chapel Steps stand above Lower Street in the foreground.

By the 1920s the view from Shepherds Hill had changed dramatically compared with twenty years before. Many new houses had been built in Haslemere Garden Suburb including Bridge Street, Popes Mead (centre) and Field Way (centre left). Close to the school were the Haslemere Hall, the first fire station which is now the Youth Art Centre, and more houses in Chestnut Avenue. However, in the distance there were still open fields beyond the school and in High Lane.

Haslemere School was built in 1899 at the end of Chestnut Avenue and opened for the first pupils, who were all boys transferred from the National School in Church Hill, in April 1900. It was built on land donated by Miss Hesse and the initial cost of £3,723 was paid for by public subscription. The building was extended in 1904, and again in 1908, increasing the original accommodation from 220 to 330 pupils which allowed the girls to move from the old National School. The piles of bricks show where work was about to start in about 1906 on the houses to the left of Chestnut Avenue. In 1968 a new Church of England Middle School was built in Derby Road and children of this age group moved there from the old school. In 1944 the school in Derby Road became an all through Primary School and the infants were transfered here from Chestnut Avenue in September 1994. The old building was sold and is now a private nursery school.

A group of girls from Class 1 at Haslemere School, c. 1910. The teacher on the right was also a member of the Haslemere Institute where he was a keen billiards player (see p. 113). The school hall was used for many other activities. Pantomimes, plays and musicals were performed on the stage before the Haslemere Hall was built.

This postcard view of Popes Mead was sent in 1905. The area in the foreground had already been set out for the next stage of the development around Bridge Road and West Street. Beyond, and to the right, is the headmaster's house at the new school in Chestnut Avenue, just visible before more houses and the Haslemere Hall were built during the following decade.

This fine Georgian house in Tanners Lane was probably built by William Bristow who was a leather tanner but by 1910 it was the Oaklands Hotel. A room here was used as St Gilbert's Catholic church until 1925 when Our Lady of Lourdes church was built in Derby Road. Father Hyland from Godalming was the parish priest until the early 1920s. Oaklands is now the nucleus of a group of retirement homes built in the gardens that once filled the area between Tanners Lane and the railway line.

Oaklands Nursery was owned for much of the early twentieth century by Mr G. Larson and produced tomatoes, cucumbers, grapes and flowers in large glasshouses to the east of Tanners Lane. Inside the tomato houses the plants were grown in individual raised boxes. The fruit hung down from the very tall plants which were grown across the roof and tied into place using raffia tape, a bundle of which is hanging from the left-hand man's waist. Locally made besom or birch brooms were used to sweep the central pathways. Produce from the nursery was sold in a small shop in Tanners Lane – about where the car park entrance is now.

Several estate agents had offices close to Haslemere station including Charles Bridger & Son who were established in 1856. Standing in the doorway in the early 1900s were Mr S. Kevan and Mr Bridger; the man on the pavement is not known. Across the road Mr Voice, a local jobmaster (operator of horse-drawn passenger vehicles) was probably waiting for passengers from the next train. If they were visitors to the area they might have stayed in apartments run by his wife. These were at Barrington House, the family home in St Christophers Road, next door to the building where Mr Voice kept his carriages; it is now used by the Haslemere Wardrobe.

Tudor House stands on the north side of Lower Street, between the railway station and Tanners Lane, and is one of the very few sixteenth-century buildings still remaining in Haslemere. Originally known as Sheepskin House, it almost certainly was connected with the tanneries nearby that gave their name to the lane. During the twentieth century it has been used as offices, a tea shop and for the sale of antiques. The eastern end, with its hipped roof, has been obscured completely since around 1900 by the building where Mr Knights had a printers and stationery shop for many years. Both of these buildings have now been adapted to provide housing.

Evennett's office was in a small building, now gone, opposite Charles Bridger & Son at Haslemere station. Mr Evennett also had an office in Farnham and the posters outside were advertising houses for sale there as well as at Shortfield, Liphook, Hindhead and in Haslemere. In case you needed financial help to make your purchase the Capital & Counties Bank was right next door.

The proprietor of the Railway Hotel on the left, soon after 1900, was C.T. Castleman. The buildings visible just beyond the hotel were a motor garage, operated later in the 1930s by Messrs Burrows and Paine. Across the forecourt of the station, behind the gas lamp, was the newly-built house of the stationmaster who was Mr C. Penney at the beginning of the century. Before this house was built a hoop shaver's shed stood there, noticed in 1897 by Mr Harry Oliver when he first came to the town (see p. 52). Mr Oliver was for many years the compiler and publisher of the *Haslemere Guide*.

Most buildings in Kings Road have changed very little since about 1912 when the shops there included a milliners run by Madam Marie, Caesar's Restaurant, the Kings Road post office where Miss Ticehurst was sub-postmistress, and a private temperance hotel on the corner of Longdene Road. Just visible in the distance is the stubby chimney of the gasworks. The Methodist church, between Kings Road and Lower Road, obscures the New Educational Hall that was used for public meetings and exhibitions. Here too the Microscope and Natural History Society, founded in 1888, met regularly and proved so popular that membership rose to over 450 within ten years.

Three

Getting Around

The railway line from London to Portsmouth via Haslemere was opened by the London & South Western Railway Company on 1 January 1859, the final link between Godalming and Havant having been completed in 1858. At first there were only four trains per day each way on a single track, but this was widened during the 1870s and two-way traffic commenced on 1 March 1879. By the time of this picture, of weekend visitors returning to London on a Monday morning around 1920, it is obvious how popular rail travel had become, and the effect that this would have on Haslemere and the surrounding villages. Also, by then, the number of trains per day had increased enabling some people to travel to work daily. But the greatest change came in 1937 when the line was electrified and up to three trains per hour ran in each direction – the age of commuting to work had really begun.

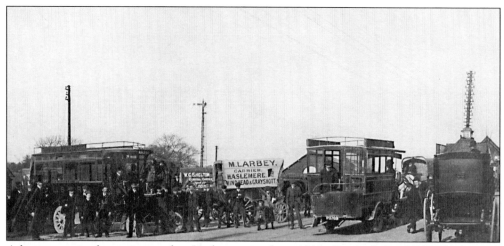

A busy scene in the station yard at Haslemere in about 1912. On the left a 24HP Thornycroft bus belonging to the London & South Western Railway Company was about to depart to Farnham. The horse-drawn wagons in the centre belonged to local carriers W.C. Shelton of East Street (Petworth Road) and M. Larbey of Clay Hill (Wey Hill). The bus on the right (rear view) was a Commer, registration number P3759, bought originally by Ben Chandler of the Royal Huts Hotel (see opposite), but he sold it to the railway company in July 1912. Just over a year later, in October 1913, it became part of Aldershot & District Traction Company. Within two years Mr Larbey's business had also become part of this rapidly expanding transport company.

L. & S.W.R. Motor Bus Service.—Single Journey Fares.

FROM	Farnham (Bush Hotel).	Farnham Station.	Bourne.	Frensham Mill Bridge or Schools.	Frensham Pond.	Churt Post Office.	Hindhead Golf Club.	Hindhead Beacon Hotel or Huts Hotel.	Nutcombe Lane.	Haslemere Station.
Farnham (Bush Hotel) ..	—	3d.	3d.	6d.	9d.	1/-	1/3	1/6	1/9	2/-
Farnham (Station) ..	3d.	—	3d.	6d.	9d.	1/-	1/3	1/6	1/9	2/-
Bourne	3d.	3d.	—	3d.	6d.	9d.	1/-	1/3	1/6	1/9
Frensham (Mill Bridge or Schools)	6d.	6d.	3d.	—	3d.	6d.	9d.	1/-	1/3	1/6
Frensham Pond	9d.	9d.	6d.	3d.	—	3d.	6d.	9d.	1/-	1/3
Churt Post Office	1/-	1/-	9d.	6d.	3d.	—	3d.	6d.	9d.	1/-
Hindhead Golf Club ..	1/3	1/3	1/-	9d.	6d.	3d.	—	3d.	6d.	9d.
Hindhead (Beacon Hotel or Huts Hotel) ..	1/6	1/6	1/3	1/-	9d.	6d.	3d.	—	3d.	6d.
Nutcombe Lane	1/9	1/9	1/6	1/3	1/-	9d.	6d.	3d.	—	3d.
Haslemere Station ..	2/-	2/-	1/9	1/6	1/3	1'-	9d.	6d.	3d.	—

Charges for Luggage accompanying Passengers:—
Small Articles, 2d. per package; Large or Bulky Articles, 4d. per package.

The price of a single ticket on the London & South Western Railway Company buses from Haslemere to Farnham, and the various fare stages between, were shown in the 2nd Edition of the *Haslemere & Hindhead Guide*, published in 1911 by Harry J.R. Oliver. This route, begun in 1905, was later taken over by the Aldershot & District Traction Company. The No. 19 bus still follows a very similar route today, although now it terminates in Aldershot.

An impressive range of cars and buses ply their trade outside the Royal Huts Hotel at Hindhead, *c.* 1910. The vehicles at either end were operated from the hotel by Ben Chandler and provided a service to Grayshott and Haslemere – but this was soon to change ownership (see opposite).

Business for local hotels, cafés and public houses increased greatly when motorized charabancs started to bring visitors regularly to the district. This large group was pictured outside the Seven Thorns by Hodgson & Martin of Bramshott Chase whose cameras recorded many of the tourists who came to this once attractive spot, probably on their way to Portsmouth or Southsea on a day trip (see p. 118).

On 18 September 1926 an Aldershot to Haslemere bus carrying thirty passengers went out of control at Hindhead due to a steering defect. The 32-seat Daimler bus was driven by Mr Waybourne and ran up the bank and overturned. Many of the passengers were hurt slightly but two people sustained more serious injuries and were detained in hospital. Sadly Arthur Sumster, who suffered a broken neck in the accident, died a few weeks later.

After the accident escape through the normal entrance door was not possible as the bus lay on its offside. Driver Waybourne and Conductor Owens rescued passengers by opening the roll-top roof. The accident appears to have happened in the Tilford Road, close to Highcombe Edge and opposite the top end of the Golden Valley.

The Hindhead Garage of the Aldershot & District Traction Company in the 1960s with an AEC Rehance bus bodied by Park Royal about to depart on tour to Widecombe-in-the-Moor in Devonshire. The garage opened in 1931 to replace the original depot at Wey Hill, Haslemere, a building where Clement windows are now manufactured. Service buses operated for the last time from the Hindhead Garage on Saturday 28 October 1995.

Before the centre of Haslemere High Street was made-up and the present traffic system introduced buses used to terminate in front of the town hall. In about 1925 Mr J.H. Stedman, who lived in Marleycombe Road at Camelsdale, began the Progressive Bus Service from Haslemere to Hammer Vale. This bus was his first vehicle, possibly a small Dodge chassis with the body built locally and with a rear-opening door. In 1935 he bought a Dennis Ace with twenty seats which was sold in May 1948. At the same time he sold his bus service to the Aldershot & District Traction Company.

This Burrell traction engine belonging to George Ewen of Petersfield had been hauling bricks, 6,000 at a time, from West Liss to a building site in Lion Lane. On Monday 25 June 1906 it is thought that while the driver Alfred Privett, his mate William Dennis and Mr Ewen's son stopped for refreshments, some children had removed the safety key from the differential pin. As the Burrell approached Shottermill railway bridge it gained speed, hit the bank and overturned with a very noisy loss of steam. Fortunately none of the three people were injured seriously but the engine was so badly damaged that Mr Ewen sold it back to Burrell to be rebuilt. He had bought the engine at Smithfield Show in 1895 for £580 – he only received £80 for its remains.

Local buses had to be diverted via Weydown Road while repairs were made to Foster's Bridge in December 1955. Note the large sign that used to require conductors of double deck omnibuses to alight and check that the road was clear before proceeding through the centre of the arch.

Four

Haslemere Again

Looking along the Petworth Road, *c.* 1908. At this time it was called East Street but in the eighteenth century had been known as Cow Street. The houses with their gables facing the road were for many years part of Stone's china shop, which had begun next door to the Olde Curiosity Shoppe of Mr Brunel Hoyes in Lower Street (see p. 24). Beyond is the White Lion Inn and Pannell's shoe shop. By 1936 this was the East Street Café which continued into the 1980s as Stafford's sweet shop. The early milk float was delivering straight from the dairy in large churns.

A group of Edwardian ladies and gentlemen outside the White Lion Inn in Petworth Road. The men on the right were probably farmers or other local businessmen who usually wore bowler hats as an indication of their status in local society. In 1900 this public house was listed as the Lion Inn where M. Bicknell was the landlord. During the First World War and into the 1920s the publican was George Benwell and it was called the White Lion, a name that continued until its closure in the 1960s. It has since been an antiques and craft centre, offices and a fashion shop.

The almshouses along the Petworth Road, c. 1890. Two pairs of almshouses were built in 1676 with funds collected from the High Street market authorized by the Royal Charter of 1596. The third pair of cottages in the foreground were built in 1886 and paid for by Mr Stewart Hodgson.

Sir Jonathan Hutchinson was born at Selby, Yorkshire in 1828. After leaving school he studied medicine, at first in York and then at St Bartholomew's Hospital, London, from where he qualified as a surgeon in 1850. He continued his career in London and in 1859 was appointed Assistant Surgeon to the London Hospital, becoming Surgeon in 1873. During his medical career he wrote numerous scientific papers and several text books including an Atlas of Clinical Surgery. In his spare time he was a keen naturalist, coming to the Haslemere area in about 1875 where he bought Weydown Farm in Bunch Lane and a house he called Inval. It was here in 1888 that a small wooden building was built to house his growing collection of specimens and artefacts – the embryo that was to develop and become the Haslemere Educational Museum.

Sir JONATHAN HVTCHINSON

Sir Jonathan Hutchinson built his new museum in 1894 to a design by his son Herbert, both to house his own large collection and to provide space for his weekend lectures to the local people – thus the Haslemere Educational Museum was born. The museum opened in 1895 and soon needed a curator. Sir Jonathan appointed Mr E.W. Swanton to the post in November and he remained with the museum for the next fifty years. In 1919 the Management Committee, set up after the death of Sir Jonathan, decided that new and larger premises in the town centre were needed (see p. 20). After the move to The Lodge in 1926 the buildings at Museum Hill remained empty for three years before becoming the offices of Haslemere Urban District Council.

A two-wheeled cart cautiously descends the steeper part of Shepherds Hill in 1880. The raised pavement and cottages to the left remain little changed today. However, the tile hung building to the right was demolished in the 1930s. The Empire, the first cinema in the town, was built in the gap between these two groups of cottages and opened in September 1914. The stage door was in Shepherds Hill but the public entrance was in Lower Street. It was owned by W. & E. Oldershaw who had also opened a second cinema, the Regal, on Wey Hill only a month later. But the Regal was fitted with sound equipment whereas the Empire only ever showed silent films. This difference led to dwindling audiences at the latter cinema which closed by the late 1920s and was converted into flats.

The bottom part of Shepherds Hill in 1887 was very narrow. During the latter part of the eighteenth and the early nineteenth centuries it had been wide enough for the coach from London to Chichester to pass. However, with the arrival of more traffic and larger motorized vehicles in the twentieth century a wider road was needed. By the late 1930s all the buildings on the left and the lower cottages on the right had been demolished.

As Haslemere expanded in the early 1900s the fields south of the town, once part of Half Moon Farm, were generally covered by large and well-spaced houses, A development by Sir Jonathan Hutchinson included these pairs of semi-detached villas built in about 1905 in Hill Road. The houses had fine views towards the hills of Hindhead to the north and the hockey club pitch to the south. On the death of Sir Jonathan the whole estate was auctioned in July 1914, a sale which included building land in nearby Old Haslemere Road, the Old Water Tower Field, that became Haslemere Recreation Ground after the First World War.

Looking towards the town from below St Bartholomew's church around 1914 the postcard photographer saw a view now hidden by houses and trees. In the middle distance stands the newly-built Haslemere Hall. The nearer houses in Bridge Road and Field Way form part of the new Garden Suburb, developed by a Tenants Committee led by the Revd Aitken, who had succeeded Sanders Etheridge at St Bartholomew's. This committee helped provide affordable housing to rent for small families. The site, which had been rather marshy land, was crossed by a footpath to the church, now remembered in the names Field Way and Pathfields.

Lythe Hill House was built on the site of Denbigh House at Haste Hill by Mr James Stewart Hodgson in the late 1860s. This engraving of the front entrance dates from about 1900, shortly before the house and surrounding estate of about 1,500 acres (600 hectares) was purchased by wealthy industrialist Mr (later Sir) Richard Garton. This estate included several other properties including Clammer Hill Farm, Lythe Hill Farm, West End Farm, the old school at Ansteadbrook and the Almshouse Cottages. Lythe Hill was built in red brick with terracotta dressings and panels. The wall on the left, between the entrance lodge and the imposing archway leading to the gardens, was decorated with a sculptured panel in red brick of a stag hunt. During the Second World War and later the house was used by the Royal Navy. It was destroyed by fire in 1977 while undergoing renovation work.

This wide-open expanse of heathland on Blackdown around 1900 would have been typical of the area where Lord Tennyson used to walk from Aldworth. It shows how much the vegetation has changed during the last century to the detriment of some scarce animals and birds. The National Trust are now trying to open-up the area once again, gradually removing invading pines and birch scrub, to encourage the return of plants and animals that depend on an open heathland habitat, an increasingly rare resource in southern England.

Alfred Lord Tennyson, the great Victorian Poet Laureate, came to live at his new home Aldworth in 1868 four years after he first visited Haslemere. His main reason for living in isolation on Blackdown during the summer months was to avoid the public, his fans, and find peace and quiet to write his poems. He mixed very little with local people, although he did sometimes visit the shop of antiquity dealer Peter Aylwin in the High Street, and also the Wheatsheaf at Grayswood where he reputedly joined the locals for a pint and, no doubt, a large pipe of his favourite tobacco.

Aldworth was designed for Tennyson by a young architect, James Knowles, who was later knighted. More famous perhaps for designing the layout of Leicester Square, he was also a founder and editor of *The Nineteenth Century* in which he opposed the building of a Channel Tunnel. The foundation stone at Aldworth was laid on 23 April 1868 and the ten-bedroomed house was completed the following year. A contemporary account published in 1877 describes the modern Gothic House as being in admirable taste, 'with wide mullion windows, many-angled oriels in shadowy recesses, and domes where bables and pinnacles break the sky-line picturesquely.' During the next two decades Aldworth was visited by many famous people, although some locals did not apparently know whose home it was. Tennyson died at Aldworth on 6 October 1892 and his final journey from the house to Westminster Abbey began at dusk on a farm cart that carried him to Haslemere station.

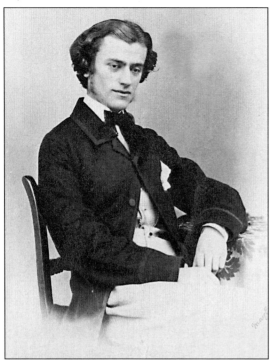

Sanders Etheridge was a young undergraduate at Cambridge in 1857 and probably quite unaware of the changes he would be bringing to Haslemere in the future. When the Revd Hesse retired in 1869 he came to the town, together with his wife Ada, and became the first rector of the new parish of Haslemere when this was separated from Chiddingfold. During the next twenty-eight years the Revd Etheridge was very involved in the new parish. Early changes included building a rectory at the corner of Three Gates Lane, a house later called Sadlers, and his involvement in the almost complete reconstruction of the parish church (see below). After Ada died in 1893 he married again in 1896 and left Haslemere the following year. However, he returned to the town when he retired and lived at Courtsmount until he died in 1912.

St Bartholomew's church about ten years after the almost complete reconstruction carried out during 1870-71. Soon after this, in 1888, a new south aisle was added to provide seating for another 120 people, needed because the local population increase had led to larger congregations, a situation that was to be further alleviated in 1903 when the church of St Christopher was built near Wey Hill.

The National School next to St Bartholomew's church was built in 1865. After several alterations and extensions the number of pupils reached almost 200 in the late 1890s. An influx of extra infant pupils, who had been taught in the town hall, arrived in 1900 when the new school for boys was opened. Soon after, the girls were also moved to Chestnut Avenue but the infants stayed at the old National School until the 1960s.

This group of pupils at the National School, Church Hill, featured on a postcard written to 'Grannie', a Mrs Austin at Worthing, in May 1913. These twenty boys and seventeen girls were infants in Year or Form II. Note the lace collars a few of the boys were wearing, a fashion belonging more to the latter part of the nineteenth century than the end of the Edwardian era.

This group of bell ringers at St Bartholomew's church in 1897 may well have been photographed by George West when the bells were rung to commemorate the Diamond Jubilee of Queen Victoria. They were, left to right, back row: F. Lamboll, H. Carpenter, E. Enticknap, H. Green. Front row: F. Egerton, T. Lamboll, J. Wakeford, W. Young.

The Revd Sanders Etheridge (centre) in 1884 with the choir outside the south porch of St Bartholomew's church.

Five

People at Work

Lowder Mill in Bell Vale Lane was powered by water from the tributary of the River Wey that rises on the western slopes of Blackdown. It is shown as a corn mill on late nineteenth-century maps. However, this group of workers in about 1880 include a cooper (second left) working on iron-bound barrels that would have been used for the storage of liquids. There was also a brewery in Bell Vale at this time – perhaps there was some connection between the two businesses? The old mill building is now part of a private house.

Puttick's Mill Foundry was almost certainly between the present-day Foundry Lane and Kings Road, about where St George's Hall and the old Dye House were later built on the south side of the road. In August 1876 there was still the 'shadow' of a water wheel visible on the wall behind the short ladder. The 1886 Ordnance Survey map showed two buildings, close together, with a leat carrying water to them from the stream near Foster's Bridge. From the mill wheel the water ran away into the stream towards Sicklemill. This is now piped below the small side road of houses, built where the first Haslemere sewage works was sited and, later, a builder's yard used by Riley & Whishaw. The approach road to the foundry led from the old coach road (see p. 100) that crossed the railway line through a crossing gate at the corner of St Christophers Road. At this time there was not a continuous road through on the present line of Kings Road. It is not known when the foundry closed but William Puttick was listed at the Lion Foundry, Shottermill, perhaps near Lion Green, in a later nineteenth-century trades directory. Perhaps this was the same family but not at the Kings Road site.

Haslemere Weaving Industry, King's Rd., Haslemere.

As part of the late nineteenth-century revival of peasant arts and crafts in Britain the Weaving House in Kings Road was built in 1898 by Joseph King. His wife Maud and her sister Ethel Blount, whose husband Godfrey played a leading role in this revival, employed local girls to weave linen and cotton materials which were then used to make children's frocks, bonnets, and other decorative or useful articles for the household. Lessons were given in spinning and weaving. The Weaving House has recently undergone extensive renovation work.

Eric Smithers in June 1924 with the one ton Model T Ford lorry that his father, Edward, had imported from America two years earlier. The firm of E. Smithers and Sons was founded in the early 1900s when Edward returned from serving on a troopship during the Boer War. He was joined by his sons, Edward who was killed on active service in 1916, Eric in about 1917, and Harold on return from duty in the Queen's Regiment. In 1926 they moved the entire contents of Haslemere Museum from Museum Hill to the High Street without a single breakage. The two brothers continued as local carriers until about 1959 when, sadly, Harold died at the wheel of a lorry while driving down Wey Hill. Eric then sold the business.

The Atherfield clay found at Hammer is very suitable for the manufacture of bricks and tiles. There had been a small brickworks there during the nineteenth century which John Grover purchased and expanded in the early 1900s using experienced workers brought from Kent. A large proportion of the bricks manufactured were used in the rapid expansion of housing around Hammer and Camelsdale, as well as for larger buildings including the imposing block of shops and flats, originally known as Electra House, at the top of Wey Hill. Employees at Hammer around 1924 were, left to right, back row: Bert Knowles, Albert Keemar, Vic Etherington, Ted Denyer, Arthur Etherington, Albert Luff, Bill Winch, Len Moorey, George Saunders, Gough White, Bill Saunders, Tuggy Boxall, Arthur Wheeler. Second row: Bert Brunt, Fred Clark, Tim Hoy, Reg Thayre, Ernie Ryman, Reg Sutton, George White, Bill Boyce, Frank Denyer, Noah Moorey, Walt Hunt, John Weeks, Albert Hill, George Puttock (with shovel). Third row: Bill Wheeler, Reuben Moorey, Tom White, Arthur Gauntlett, Jack White, Len Young, Caleb Hammond, Harry Green, Sam Ward, Abraham Brunt, Ben Keemar. Seated on the ground: George (Digger) Silk, Wesley Puttock, Percy Puttock, Ernie Bradburn, Harry Ridout, -?-, Alf Walters, Eddie Keemar.

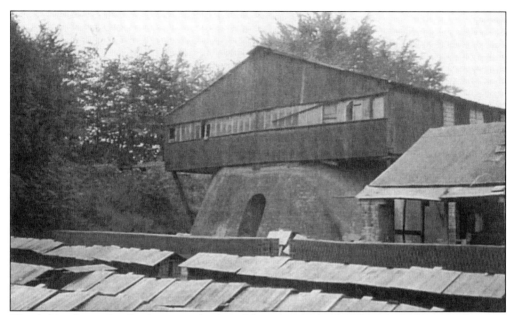

The kiln where the bricks were fired at Hammer, with the drying shed perched rather precariously on top, was photographed in July 1937 by Miss N. Massy who was helping Mr E.W. Swanton, curator at Haslemere Museum, to record the many small brickfields around the area before they all disappeared.

By 1936 the supply of extractable clay at Hammer was exhausted and the new owners, the Nutbourne Brick Company, were only making bricks locally at Hambledon, near Witley. But they continued until 1938 to use the old brickworks as a store from where bricks could be distributed to local builders. After the Second World War the clay pit was used as a landfill site for rubbish.

Much of the woodlands surrounding Haslemere were coppiced and supported a range of local underwood industries well into the twentieth century. These included charcoal burners, broom squires making besoms, wood turners such as W. Bridger, Thomas Gibbs and Charles Greenway listed in an 1868 trade directory, and hoop shavers. The latter split hazel, ash or chestnut rods to make barrel hoops of various lengths. These were used to hold together barrels which were not watertight but were used to store and transport products such as salted herrings, potatoes and for the export of pottery from Staffordshire. Usually hoop shavers worked in the woods alone but Harry Oliver mentioned a hoop shed at Haslemere station in 1897 (see p. 30). Nowadays most chestnut coppice is used by the fencing industry which developed in the early twentieth century to utilise a resource that was becoming neglected.

Old Gale, the shepherd from Inval bringing a flock of sheep down into Bunch Lane. During the nineteenth century, and earlier, sheep grazed on the heathlands around Hindhead. At this time much of the area now covered by secondary woodland was fields or open moorland. Even birds like black grouse were found on the heather moors before land enclosures led eventually to much building development around Hindhead, Grayshott and Beacon Hill.

Six

Hindhead and Beacon Hill

The Royal Huts Hotel, perhaps the best-known landmark in twentieth-century Hindhead, although better known during the last twenty years as the Happy Eater, was demolished in April 2001 to make way for a development of houses and flats on the corner between the Portsmouth Road (A3) and the road to Farnham. In the early days of motoring the hotel was owned by Ben Chandler, who had taken it over in 1893. He opened a garage alongside, which subsequently grew into the Hindhead Engineering Works after it moved to the Guildford side of the crossroads, a position where there is still a BMW garage today. The position of the hotel on such a busy road junction made this a favourite spot for patrolmen from both the RAC and the AA to wait in the hope of recruiting new members.

One of the better-known people to be attracted to Hindhead at the end of the nineteenth century was Sir Arthur Conan Doyle. His house, Undershaw, was built in 1898 between the Haslemere and Portsmouth Roads, in a wonderful position at the top of Nutcombe Valley. Here he wrote some of the later Sherlock Holmes adventures. In 1902 he purchased a motor car, one of the first at Hindhead.

Arthur Conan Doyle was knighted in 1902. Some three years later he entertained sailors from the French Fleet who had asked if they could visit him at Undershaw while on their way back from London to rejoin their ship at Portsmouth. Unfortunately, no pictures have been found of this event and the crowds that gathered to see the great writer and his visitors. Following the death of Lady Conan Doyle in 1906 he remarried a year later and left Undershaw to live at Crowborough, Sussex where he died in 1930.

Post Office Corner was built by Walter Rollason at the end of the nineteenth century as Hindhead became an important focus for visitors. Mr Rollason, and later his nieces the Misses E. and D. Rollason, sold many postcards that have left an important pictorial record of changes around Hindhead during the first fifty years of the last century. Now the old building is empty, somewhat dilapidated and under threat of demolition to improve traffic flow at this busy junction. Such is progress – the very cars that brought increased trade and prosperity to the area are now responsible for its destruction. (Postscript: The building was demolished in October 2001.)

An advertisement in the 1903 edition of the *Homeland Handbook*. The Refreshment Rooms were next door to the post office and run by Walter Rollason's two nieces.

W. ROLLASON,

𝕳igh-class 𝕮onfectioner,

THE HINDHEAD REFRESHMENT ROOMS.

GOOD ACCOMMODATION FOR CYCLISTS.
PARTIES CATERED FOR.

MINERAL WATERS, ICES,
FANCY PASTRY, &c. **LARGE TEA ROOM.**

Selection of Views of the Neighbourhood.

A CHOICE COLLECTION OF FANCY GOODS AND
TOYS FOR PRESENTS.

One of the larger hotels built as Hindhead developed in 1898 was the Beacon in Tilford Road. Around the hotel there were extensive gardens where salad crops and vegetables were grown for use in the hotel kitchens. There was even an observatory dome above the roof on the left. Changes in the way we have taken our holidays since the 1950s led to a decline in visitors to the area. The Beacon, like most other local hotels, was affected badly. When the doors finally closed it became a training centre for Lloyds Bank. After this training centre closed the old hotel was demolished in 2006 and flats and houses were built on the site.

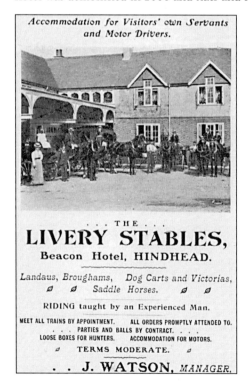

Accommodation for Visitors' own Servants and Motor Drivers.

. . . THE . . .
LIVERY STABLES,
Beacon Hotel, HINDHEAD.

Landaus, Broughams, Dog Carts and Victorias,
Saddle Horses.

RIDING taught by an Experienced Man.

MEET ALL TRAINS BY APPOINTMENT.   ALL ORDERS PROMPTLY ATTENDED TO.
. . . PARTIES AND BALLS BY CONTRACT. . . .
LOOSE BOXES FOR HUNTERS.   ACCOMMODATION FOR MOTORS.
TERMS MODERATE.

. . J. WATSON, *MANAGER.*

An advertisement from the *Homeland Handbook* to 'The Hill Country of the Surrey Borderland', Haslemere and Hindhead, published in 1903.

During the 1930s many of the businesses which prospered were catering for the needs of the numerous visitors who came to see the wild beauty of the Hindhead Commons and to visit Gibbet Hill where, in 1786, three men had been executed for the murder of a sailor whose body they had then thrown into the Devil's Punch Bowl. On the extreme left the Sally Lunn provided both accommodation and a restaurant. Nearer the crossroads was the Queen of Hearts, known originally as the Hindhead Refreshment Rooms (see previous page), which was advertised prominently on a gable-end across the road. Along the north side of the Portsmouth Road were two banks, the pharmacy of E.H. Conduit, an ice cream parlour, estate agents C. Bridger and Cubitt & West, and even a showroom for the Haslemere & District Gas Company.

The Punchbowl Inn originated as a public house serving alcoholic drinks but by around 1920 it had become a temperance house. During the 1930s it was run by Miss Francis Kennedy as the Punchbowl Café and Guest House. After it was demolished the name transferred to the hotel next door, known originally as Thorshill. The site of the old Punchbowl Inn is now a petrol station.

This radar pylon dating from the Second World War remained as a prominent landmark on Gibbet Hill, just south of the summit, until it was demolished in 1957. There had been three of these originally between the Devils Punch Bowl Hotel and Gibbet Hill. A fourth pylon stood close to the road on the southern edge of the Devil's Punch Bowl.

Hindhead and Beacon Hill Home Guard were part of No. 3 Platoon, E (Surrey) Company, 2nd Battalion (The Queen's Regiment). Seen around 1940 at the rear of the playing fields, in an area known as Gravel Hanger, were, left to right ,back row: Charlie Woods, Henry Woods, Johnny Reed, Doug Palliaster, Jack Cooper. Front row: Ernie Groves, Frank Taylor, Norman Birch, Ted Wright, Stanley Perkins, Arthur Bateman, Archie Cooper, Lionel Buckingham. Sadly Doug Palliaster was later killed while on active service in a submarine.

The custom-built Golden Hind Café opened in 1930 but struggled to make a living for its first owner, who was eventually declared bankrupt in 1932. Six years later K. Partington was much more successful; besides the café, accommodation was also available for visitors to the area. Perhaps some were attracted to stay by the large model of Sir Francis Drake's Golden Hind that was displayed on a post at the roadside.

Inside, the Golden Hind was typical of the 1930s with potted palms, gateleg tables and wheelback or Windsor chairs. Inclusive terms were two and a half guineas weekly to include breakfast, lunch and supper. Special weekend terms for Saturday supper until breakfast on Monday were £1 inclusive, while bed and breakfast cost 6s.

HINDHEAD & CHURT

IN THE PARISHES OF FRENSHAM & HEADLEY,

ON THE BORDERS OF SURREY AND HAMPSHIRE,

About 6 Miles from Farnham and 4 from Haslemere Stations, on the L. & S.W. Railway.

The Particulars, Plans and Conditions of Sale of

VALUABLE FREEHOLD ESTATE

OF

580 ACRES,

SITUATE AT CHURT, BARFORD & HINDHEAD,

IN THE PARISHES OF FRENSHAM & HEADLEY,

IN THE COUNTIES OF SURREY & HAMPSHIRE,

COMPRISING A CHARMING

RESIDENTIAL PROPERTY

OF ABOUT

121 ACRES,

With House, Grounds, Stabling and Heath Lands, including Two of the famed

DEVIL'S JUMPS;

ALSO

THE FARMS & HOMESTEADS,

Known as Red Hearne, Green Cross, Hatch and Kitt's Farms,

15 COTTAGES,

WATER CORN MILL WITH MILL HOUSE & MALT KILN

THE BARFORD PONDS,

SITUATE IN WHITMORE VALE,

Where excellent Trout Fishing is obtained; also about

180 ACRES OF HEATH LAND,

ON HINDHEAD COMMON,

700 feet above Sea level, having Extensive Frontages to good Roads,

Which will be offered for Sale by Auction, by

Mr. J. ALFRED EGGAR

(by order of W. Ansell, Esq.)

AT THE MART, TOKENHOUSE YARD, LONDON,

On MONDAY, OCT. 27th, 1890,

AT TWO O'CLOCK PRECISELY,

IN 16 LOTS.

Particulars with Plans and Conditions of Sale may be obtained of Messrs. G. F. HUDSON MATTHEWS & Co., 32, Queen Victoria Street, London, E.C.; at the Mart; and of the Auctioneer, Farnham and Alton.

JOHN NICHOLS, Printer and Binder, Borough, Farnham.

An important sale of land to the north of Hindhead in 1890 included much of the heathland where Beacon Hill was developed during the next twenty years. Of particular importance was Lot 11 which was described as a valuable enclosure of freehold heathland containing about 76 acres (33 hectares) and having extensive frontages to the roads leading from Farnham and Frensham to Haslemere. It was also said to be 'almost 700 feet above sea level' (about 210 metres) with extensive views 'including Windsor Castle and Haslemere' – it must have been a very clear day when the estate agent wrote this description!

Beacon Hill Road in about 1910 still looked like a very new development on the open heathland site which had been sold twenty years earlier. Shops here included the Beacon Hill Dairy of H. Madgwick & Son on the left with Grinstead Brothers next door. Just past the horse and cart was the post office where Harold Chapman was postmaster. At that time the mail was collected three times daily on weekdays and once on Sunday afternoon.

The butcher at Headley Road, Grayshott was H. Mitchell who saw the growth of Beacon Hill as an area into which he could expand his business. In 1904 his delivery cart was stopped outside the newly-built houses in what was then known as Farnham Road; that name was changed soon after to Tilford Road.

The first butchers shop of Grinstead Brothers in Beacon Hill Road, c. 1915. This was one of several new businesses that soon provided competition for the shopkeepers from Grayshott and Hindhead. By 1921 Grinstead Brothers had moved to Southdown House in Beacon Hill Road. Later in 1936 Mr A. Parham was the proprietor at this butchery. The original shop is now a private house called Laurel Cottage.

The Temple of the Four Winds was built as a shooting box in 1910 by Lord Pirrie, owner of the extensive Witley Park Estate, chairman of the Harland & Wolff shipyard in Belfast and a director of the White Star Shipping Line. It was positioned between Gibbet Hill and High Button at the western edge of his estate. In 1959 the roof was destroyed by vandals. Further structural deterioration over the next few years left the building in such a precarious condition that the Hindhead Management Committee of the National Trust decided demolition was the only option. This was carried out in 1966 by the 1st Training Squadron of the Royal Engineers. Today only the floor remains to mark the spot where it once stood.

Seven

At Your Service

During the first half of the twentieth century Haslemere Urban District Council were responsible for the roads within the town but Hambledon Rural District Council looked after the roads in the surrounding areas. This steam road roller and council workmen in 1911 were repairing the road at the bottom of Haste Hill in the days before local roads were surfaced with tarmacadam. The children were standing on a heap of roadstone, probably local chert rock, to be used for filling potholes and ruts. The cast iron plate on the roller names O. Lintott as the HRDC surveyor. It was his responsibility to maintain the roads across a wide area in south-west Surrey which included Alfold, Bramley, Chiddingfold, Cranleigh, Dunsfold, Elstead, Frensham, Hascombe, Haslemere outside the urban district, Thursley, Tilford, Witley and Wonersh. The council offices were in Shalford. The postcard showing the roller was written by Reg, perhaps one of the four workmen, who was asking Wilfred Bradley in Petersfield whether or nor 'the slides' (presumably for a magic lantern) were ready yet as he 'should like to have them for use on Coronation Day'. The card was written on 15 June 1911. Perhaps he was about to provide an entertainment at one of the local celebrations when King George V and Queen Mary were crowned on 22 June. Let's hope he saw the slides in time!

Haslemere Fire Brigade had two fire engines around 1937 called Princess Elizabeth and Princess Margaret. The third fireman on the left of the group sitting on the fire engine was Amos Chandler. The driver of the Haslemere Urban District Council ambulance, on the left, was Mr Strudwick. The chief fire officer was Captain A.N. Stratton and Mr Crick was his deputy. Other firemen present included A. Denyer, L. Furlong, R. Furlong, L. Hailey, F. Hunter, G. Joyce, S. Moorey, W.W. Strudwick (junior), Eric Venton, R. Weeks and F. Wright.

The first hospital in Haslemere was built at the top of Shepherds Hill. It was a very generous gift to the town from John Wornham Penfold and his sisters, Susanna and Kate, to celebrate the Diamond Jubilee of Queen Victoria, and was opened on 11 June 1898 by the Lord Lieutenant of Surrey. At first there were only four beds but this was soon increased to six when an extension was built. The last matron, Miss Davenport McPhee, moved to the new hospital when it opened in 1923 (see opposite).

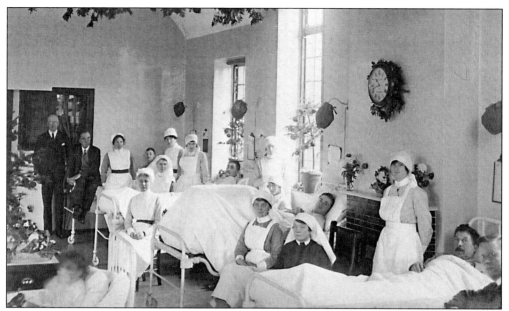

Christmas in a corner of the men's ward at Haslemere and District Hospital in the 1920s. The hospital was built in 1922 and opened by the Lord Chancellor, Viscount Cave, on 20 January 1923. It was built by Chapman, Lowry & Puttick to a design by Herbert Read FRIBA at a cost of over £35,000 which had been raised by public subscription. At first there were thirty-five beds and cots. Further work in the 1920s, including a children's ward, X-ray and massage rooms and more accommodation for nursing and domestic staff, were largely funded by the generosity of Sir Richard Garton in memory of both his grand-daughter, Miss Rachel Corbett, and his wife.

Raising money for the new hospital was a charity well supported at the Haslemere Carnival in the early 1920s. This float bears a huge sign with the legend 'The Morris Van will take a ton of money. Load it up for the Hospital'. The procession is just about to pass the drapery of Percy Horace Stone at the Broadway, premises first used by Haslemere's longest established ironmongers, Robert Miles, before they moved to West Street.

During the eighteenth and nineteenth centuries the post office occupied various addresses in East Street and the High Street. From 1895 until 1906, when the new post office was built in West Street, the postmaster was William Charman, a stationer and newsagent at the Broadway. This group of postmen are pictured outside Haslemere School on Good Friday 1904. They were, from left to right, back row: C.W. Chapman, T. Upfold, A. Gale, C. Upfold, J.J. Moore, H. Roffe, F. Coombes, T. Oakford, J. Chilton, A.V. Etherington, T. Griffin (an employee of the contractor who carried the mail from Guildford to Haslemere), E. Morley, C. Young, W.G. Moore, E. Young. Middle seated: C. Henbest, A. Boniface, L.G. Foster, W. Charman (postmaster), E.L. Jones, T. Pine. In front: E.W. Roe, A. Bicknell, T. Moorey, T. Moorey.

Hilders, the Surrey home of Lord Aberconway on the high ground between the Hindhead Road and Lion Lane, was used as an auxilliary medical hospital during the First World War. Later Hilders was the home of the Rt Hon Sir John Tudor Walters JP before becoming St Martha's Training College in the 1930s. By 1938 Sydney H. Smith had opened Branksome Hilders, a preparatory school for boys, which continued there for more than thirty years. More recently the house has been used as a training centre by Olivetti and Ericsson; it is now a De Vere conference centre.

A comic postcard from around 1916 showing a wounded soldier in his 'blues', the uniform worn by men while convalescing during the First World War. These coloured cards were overprinted with the names of various auxiliary hospitals in different parts of the country. This card was sent by Mark to Flossie in Gravesend thanking her for some books and reporting that he was very much better.

Are we Downhearted ?
NO ! Not at HILDERS.

During the First World War the Convent of the Cenacle in Headley Road, Grayshott, was used as a military hospital, thanks to the Reverend Mother and Sisters who not only provided the premises, but also helped with the cooking and other work. The Commandant was Miss Bewley, who was in charge of the nursing staff, together with other helpers from the surrounding area including Dr Lyndon, the GP from Grayshott. During 1917 and 1918 three of the nurses were, left to right: Sister Malkin, Sister Leach and Miss Kay, together with a group of their patients. The hospital closed on 14 January 1919. The convent was closed and the site redeveloped for housing in the late 1990s.

Haslemere Urban District Council still operated a 'lavender' cart to collect 'night soil' from earth closets as late as the 1960s. Here it is seen at Grove Road, Beacon Hill in July 1965 before flush toilets were fitted at Erica Cottages.

This fine body of local men and women formed No. 3 Platoon, (Haslemere) 2nd Surrey Battalion Home Guard. They were on duty in the early 1940s at Hindhead Court, a house built by Mr Kelton, father of their commanding officer. The house, now part of the Royal School, is situated between the Portsmouth Road and Hazel Grove, Hindhead. The line-up included, from left to right, back row: Ptes Worsdell, Read, R. Judge, Coles, Luff, Nash, Hill, White, Cpls Vincent, Taylor. Second row: Cpl Peskett, Pte Chegwin, Cpl Tarring, Ptes Covell, Thorne, C.A. Smith, Budd, Cpl Alcock, Pte Hannant, L/Cpt Larby. Third row: Ptes C.F. Woods, G. Walker, Telling, Woodington, Redwood, Horner, Wright, Bond, Rogers, Clements, Cpl Durrant, Ptes Horton, C.R. Smith. Front row: Pte Mercer (Croix de Guerre), L/Cpl Whitehead, Ptes Enticknap, Randall, Rooke, Mumford, Cadet Sgt Nolan, Pte A.J. Woods, L/Cpl Creasey, Ptes Johns, T.W. King, Peaty, Cpl Gould. Seated: Miss Simpson, Miss Holland, Sgt Whisker, Sgt Culver, Platoon Sgt Bloomfield, Lt Thwaites, Lt Davies, Maj. Kelton, Dr Gray, CSM Luff, Sgts Aycliffe, Ellis, Jennings, Miss Baggott, Mrs Whisker. On the ground in front: Cpl Blackwell, Pte A.H. Walker, Sgt Cook, Ptes C. King, Schilling and Buckingham.

An emergency wartime fire station was opened in 1939 at the end of Sturt Avenue, Camelsdale, close to the Water Works. It consisted of a Nissen hut and a wooden shed, built on land owned by Mr Horace Green who was the first Station Commander (extreme left). During the war there were thirty-six enlisted men stationed at Camelsdale.

The first fire-fighting vehicle at Camelsdale Auxiliary Fire Station was Mr Green's own Ford V8 motor car. This towed a pump which was being used here during a fire practice; Stuart Farm can be seen in the background. After the war Camelsdale became part of the West Sussex Fire Brigade on 1 April 1948 but was closed in 1966.

Eight

Into Sussex and Hampshire

Some rather unseasonable snow on 25 April 1908 led to this picturesque view of Oliver's Mill. This mill was used to grind grain in the nineteenth and early twentieth centuries, unlike the nearby mills owned by James Simmons that had been involved in paper making and later, at Sicklemill, the manufacture of braid to decorate uniforms. William Oliver also used wind power on the hill above Grayswood. But in 1886 the windmill at Higher Combe was pulled down and parts of the machinery were installed into the water mill where they continued to help grind corn. After working in the dry and dusty mill no doubt the miller crossed the road to the Railway Tavern, now the Mill Tavern, where the publican in 1908, George Dew, would have poured him a refreshing pint of his best ale. The outbuildings around the old tavern have long since gone. So too has the cart shed opposite the mill which was demolished in the 1960s to improve the line of the road towards Shottermill Ponds.

At the point where the three counties of Surrey, Sussex and Hampshire meet in Hammer Vale is the remains of a sluice, part of the old Pophole, or Pophall, ironworks. It is now difficult to imagine that for more than 200 years this was industrial Britain – perhaps the closest reminder being the iron railway track nearby, carrying trains from London to Portsmouth. But these came much later of course, following the discovery that iron could be smelted with coke more efficiently than with charcoal that led quickly to the transfer of the whole iron industry to the coalfield areas of the Midlands and northern England.

Hammer Lane showing the mission church that had recently been built and, in the distance, the original Prince of Wales public house, c. 1907. The landlord at this time was James Scragg, who also ran a small shop. The lady is Mrs Scragg who owned a number of properties in the lane. The church was demolished in 1965.

The new Prince of Wales pub soon after it opened in 1927. At this time the landlord was William Scragg, probably a relative of James who had been the publican twenty years earlier (see opposite).

Hammer Vale Pottery,

Haslemere, Surrey.

Makers of HASLEMERE WARE.

Agents at :—	
Haslemere	ARTISTIC TILES FOR FIRE-PLACES,
Hindhead	BATH-ROOMS, etc.
Grayshott	
Chiddingfold	TERRA COTTA GARDEN WARE,
Churt	
Frensham	*Special designs and estimates on application.*
Liphook	
Godalming	
Guildford	Proprietor—
Weybridge	
Bridport	**W. W. Stallworthy**
Banbury	
Bognor	
Chipstead	Potter and
Midhurst	
Surbiton	Ceramic Craftsman.
London	

Works open to Visitors, 10 to 4-30, Saturdays, 10 to 12.

16

Hammer Vale Pottery was started in 1901 by J. Radley Young who was later joined by William Wilson Stallworthy, son of George Burnett Stallworthy, the minister at Haslemere, and later Hindhead, Congregational churches. A contemporary account in a 1903 guide reveals that the Faience and Mosaic Works was in Hammer Lane, New Haslemere (it was actually close to the railway bridge) 'where Mr Young is responsible for designing the wares that are produced principally from local materials', probably Atherfield clay from the claypit at Hammer Brickworks. By 1908 only W.W. Stallworthy is mentioned in advertisements and the pottery had closed by 1911. Few examples of the wares, which are usually marked 'W W STALLWORTHY HASLEMERE', seem to have survived.

The two ponds at Shottermill were dammed to provide a head of water for the corn mill. The road originally ran alongside the upper pond enabling the horse pulling this delivery cart from the Broadway Stores in the High Street to get a drink. Maybe even the driver was able to take the cart into the water on a hot, dry day and tighten up the spokes and felloes of the wheels. These would swell as the wood took up water and help stop the wheels rattling as the cart was driven along the unmade roads with their many potholes.

New Road, Camelsdale by 1909 showing how quickly this area was developed at the beginning of the twentieth century. Most of the houses were built with bricks supplied from the nearby Hammer Brickworks. A line of trees has been planted either side of the road. Each tree has been protected from damage by horses with a triangle of wooden posts and rails which are also covered from the ground to the second rail with rabbit netting.

The houses in Sturt Avenue were built at about the same time as those in New Road. Later, in 1939, the Camelsdale Auxiliary Fire Station was established at the end of the avenue, just across the road from Sturt Farm (see p. 70).

Camelsdale Stores was on the north side of the main road. It was one of a number of small shops that had sprung up to supply the needs of people who had moved into the new houses in the area. In a 1921 directory the proprietor, Alfred Austin, advertised the 'Highest Quality Groceries & Provisions at London Store Prices'. He also sold fruit, greengroceries, mineral waters, tobacco, patent medicines and postage stamps. The pillar box on the right was emptied three times a day every weekday!

This fine old barn once stood on the south side of Camelsdale Road, not far from the junction with Sturt Road. Although it is now gone the cottages opposite still identify the precise spot where this photograph was taken around 1904.

The road into Sussex as it was in the 1930s with Bell Vale Lane turning to the left, just over the stream from Blackdown that marks the county boundary. There used to be a brewery in Bell Vale where, in 1900, W. Kiln was perhaps the last brewer to make beer there. He may well have supplied the Sussex Bell public house that was once behind the trees on the right and where, in 1913, the landlady was Mrs Day.

Nine

Grayswood

Looking down the hill through Grayswood, c. 1904. The road had been constructed as a new toll route from Godalming in the eighteenth century. On the right a sign advertising the Wheatsheaf Inn hangs outside what is now a private house. It was in 1904 that the Surrey Public Houses Trust Co. Ltd built the new Wheatsheaf across the road. However, the presence of the sign on the right suggests that this postcard view is from a slightly earlier date, probably before the original inn where Lord Tennyson had reputedly been a customer, closed.

The new and purpose-built Grayswood post office around 1912, some two or three years after it opened with Marie Moorey as the first postmistress. At this time the office was open to customers from 9a.m. to 6.15p.m. There were three collections from the letterbox on weekdays, the last being at 6p.m., and one on Sunday morning.

All Saints' church was built in 1900-01 and consecrated by the Bishop of Winchester in February 1902. The first vicar was the Revd J.S. Leake who was instituted in 1900 and remained until the 1920s. The church was designed by Axel Hägg, a Swedish naval officer who became a church architect after settling in Britain in 1856. His grave in front of the church is marked by a tombstone decorated with a Viking ship in full sail.

Looking up the hill towards Haslemere with the Grayswood Men's Institute on the right, c. 1910. Until the end of 1904 the institute had been the village school. Just after the First World War the President of the Institute was L.N.H. Bailey, the Revd Leake was Treasurer and Mr L. Smithers was Hon Secretary. Members of the Committee included Messrs G. Clear, P. Denyer, A. Smithers, F. Puttock, F. Hack, J. Jordan, F. Patent, W. Stallard and A. Puttock.

The new Church of England school was built during 1904 and opened at 9.00a.m. on 30 January 1905 in the presence of the Revd and Mrs Leake and Mr Levi Smithers. The head teacher until 1915 was Mr H.L. Mumford who was assisted by Miss Williamson, Miss Barnfield and probationers Miss J. Jones and Miss A. Russell. There were 100 pupils registered and 97 were present on the first day. Medals were presented to twelve children for perfect attendance in the previous year. They were Andrew Bicknell, Alec Court, May Frost, Lucy Hack, Laura Smith, George Smithers, Annie, Ester and Nellie Snelling, Jessie Talman, W. Turner and Ethel Waite.

This group of very keen senior boys from Grayswood School won the District Gardening Shield in about 1912. They were left to right, back row: M. Creasy, H. Smithers, W. Ayling, E. Ashdown, G. Matthews, W. Adams. Front row: K. Lawrence, L. Randall, E. Penycate, G. Wynn, W. Baker, C. Hammond, A. Hawkins, W. Watson. At this time practical activities such as woodwork, sewing and gardening were much encouraged. The gardens behind the school were divided into many plots for both boys and girls. There was also a tool shed, seed beds, wire work for soft fruit and even a rustic fence for rambler roses. When necessary, work in the garden had priority over other lessons. For instance on 22 March 1910 the school log states that 'gardening will be taken this afternoon instead of geography and composition as several seeds need sowing before Easter Vacation'. Later, in August 1915, Mr W. Brooks from the Haslemere Horticultural Society judged the gardens (for the District Shield?) and noted that the school gardens were 'as usual very good and most of the crops looking very well and quite up to the usual standard'. He also commented that the boys 'must have all been very keen to have kept their plots so nice and tidy'.

The village pond at Grayswood was in a hollow alongside Lower Road and was a favourite place around 1910 for children to play on their way home from school. Surely many a pair of shoes needed a good clean and polish after the wearer had ventured too near the edge before going home from lessons in the afternoon.

The dividing of the ways with Lower Road going to the left past the pond, *c*. 1910. Along the Mount, which follows the route of an older track to the right from Clammer Hill, two young boys are playing with a 'soapbox' cart. At this time many items were delivered to shops in a variety of wooden barrels, crates and boxes. Those not returned by the shopkeeper were then used for storage or kindling wood; and a few even became play things.

Looking along Prestwick Lane towards Chiddingfold from the junction with Lower Road, 1904. This lane and Clammer Hill were once part of the old route to Godalming (see below). The late Victorian houses built along the section of this road known as Klondyke commemorate the 1896-98 gold rush in Alaska.

The Stroud, the large house on the right just as you leave Grayswood towards Brook, was a preparatory school for boys in the 1930s and the principal was Mr B.H. Molony. Next door the small, single-storey Stroud Cottage was built as a toll house when the new road from Godalming to Haslemere was made through Brook and Birtley in the eighteenth century. Much of the area between Witley and Haslemere is on heavy and wet clay soils which were difficult for horse-drawn vehicles to cross during the winter months. The original road approached the town from Chiddingfold via Prestwick Lane and Three Gates Lane. This new and shorter route must have improved the journey times to Haslemere from Guildford and London, as well as from Godalming.

Ten

Celebrations

King Edward VII passed through Haslemere on 3 November 1903 on his way to Lords Common, Midhurst, to lay the foundation stone of the sanatorium that is named after him. The King arrived by train at 11.55a.m. and was then driven in an open landau carriage to the ceremony, taking a route along Kings Road through Sicklemill and Sturt Road to Fernhurst. Before this visit Kings Road had been called Foundry Road or Gas-house Lane and was not the most attractive part of the town to take such an important visitor through. At Haslemere station the royal party was met by Viscount Middleton, the Lord Lieutenant of Surrey, with the Haslemere Bands playing on the platform as the train arrived. Outside the station yard there was a guard of honour with nearly 100 men of the 2nd Volunteer Brigade, the Queen's Royal West Surrey Regiment, commanded by Captain the Hon. Arthur Broderick. Children from Haslemere School were taken by the headmaster, G.H. Tyler, and the headmistress, Miss Palmer, to Foundry Meadow in Kings Road where they stood on boards to cheer as the Royal carriage passed. As the procession left the station the King bared his head to acknowledge the large crowds. Note that many of the buildings on the other side of Lower Street, opposite the station, have since been pulled down.

A great procession followed King Edward VII along Kings Road towards Midhurst in 1903 and included both the Bridger and Institute Bands; they later amalgamated and became Haslemere Band soon after the First World War. The building on the left was the gasworks. The Haslemere Gas Company was incorporated in 1868 with a nominal capital of £1,500 under the chairmanship of G. Bowlder Buckton. The Haslemere postmaster in 1868, Peter Aylwin, who was also a pharmacist and bookseller, became the first manager of the gas company. In 1917 the Limited Company was dissolved and re-incorporated as The Haslemere and District Gas Company, becoming part of the Southern Gas Board following nationalization on 1 May 1949. The old gas works was closed in 1972 when the area was converted to natural gas.

After laying the foundation stone at Midhurst the King returned to Waterloo station on a train that left Haslemere at 1.55p.m. He was accompanied on his return journey by the Lord Lieutenant of Sussex, the Marquis of Abergavenny, KG. Once again the Queen's Royal West Surrey Regiment formed a guard of honour. Shortly afterwards, on Tuesday 14 November, the High Sheriff of Surrey, Mr Walpole Greenwell, entertained the police and railway staff involved in the royal visit to dinner at the Swan Hotel.

Haslemere people celebrated the Golden Jubilee of Queen Victoria on 21 June 1887 by decorating the High Street with flags, bunting and foliage. This was evidently a topic for conversation between the men outside Alfred Softley's butchers shop. Further along the road the ladies outside Chilman's wine and spirit shop are probably also discussing the forthcoming festivities which were to include a Service of Thanksgiving, a public dinner, children's party and a beacon on Gibbet Hill at Hindhead in the evening.

Special moments in time have often been marked by large gatherings of people in the High Street. The end of the First World War was one such occasion. Peace Day was celebrated on Saturday 19 July 1919. A large arch covered in foliage, flags and bunting bridged the gap between the town hall and the corner of Petworth Road. Surely none of the young people in the crowd that day imagined another terrible conflict would begin only twenty years later, and that some of their lives would be cut short in the ultimate sacrifice for their country.

Haslemere firemen pulling the new steam pump round Penfold Corner on 1 May 1907. It had been delivered by train to the railway station and was then moved in a procession along Lower Street to the presentation ceremony in the High Street.

Mr (later Sir) Richard Garton presenting his gift of a new Shand Mason steam pump to Haslemere Fire Brigade Captain, the Earl of Altamont, on 1 May 1907. Later, in 1934, Sir Richard gave the town a new motor fire engine. Until recently a steamer, with Haslemere on the side, was on view at the Cobh Heritage Centre, near Cork in Ireland. This was not the original Haslemere machine but another, bought some time ago in Kent, and named by a signwriter some fifteen years ago.

Haslemere Carnival procession passing the Broadway in the early 1920s. The BP lorry full of revellers is about to pass Charman's shop where you could buy your daily newspaper as well as stationery, fancy goods and toys. William Charman also published a very useful and informative directory listing local businesses as well as private names and addresses. During the early 1900s his shop had also been the post office. In 1906 the present post office was built in West Street and Mr Charman continued as postmaster until he retired.

These drivers and their delivery carts from Haslemere & District Co-operative Society had gathered in the old Shottermill Recreation Ground prior to a local parade. This land had been a gift to the people of Shottermill from James Simmons whose family had owned Sickle Mill. Mr Simmons lived at Field End, the house which stood where the Waverley Locality Office is now sited. The 'Rec', where many fêtes and sporting fixtures took place, was replaced by Haslemere Swimming Pool which opened on 2 October 1971. The pool closed on 19 June 1998 to be replaced by the Herons Leisure Centre at Sicklemill which opened on 25 July 1998. A Tesco supermarket was built on the site of the old swimming pool.

A Thanksgiving Service to celebrate the Silver Jubilee of King George V and Queen Mary in 1935 took place on St Christophers Green. Here crowds of people including the territorial army, girl guides and brownies listened to the service from St Paul's Cathedral as it was broadcast via several large loud speakers. Two of these, one square and the other round, are visible just to the right of the corrugated iron buildings of William Furlonger's garage where you were able to buy an Austin car and fill it with a gallon of National Benzol petrol.

Saluting the flag at the Jubilee Thanksgiving watched by the men of the Haslemere Fire Brigade. The lesson had been read by the Revd Leonard Brook and a speech made by Admiral James, who lived at Churt and is, perhaps, better known as the little curly-haired boy who modelled for the painting 'Bubbles' by Millais, used widely as an advertisement for Pears soap. After the service the celebrations moved to Lion Green where the children were able to ride on a large and colourful merry-go-round.

Eleven

Around Wey Hill

This procession led by the Comrades of the Great War marched along Wey Hill on their way to the town centre as part of the 1919 Peace Celebrations. They passed the original Crown and Cushion public house, which was kept by Herbert Darby, but was soon to be demolished. The present Crown and Cushion dates from 1921 and was designed by Frederick Hodgson, an architect from Guildford who also planned the new police station, built in West Street in 1925. The laundry building to the right, later the Wey Hill Garage, was pulled down in the 1960s. The photographer stood on Fosters Bridge to see the whole procession. Originally this name may have referred to an earlier bridge over the small stream, a tributary of the River Wey, that now flows through a culvert under the road and the railway embankment. The land at the beginning of Kings Road, where the Three Counties church now stands, was known as Foster's Croft on a sketch plan compiled in 1867 by John Wornham Penfold from earlier tithe maps.

One of the pits that gave Wey Hill its earlier name of Clay Hill was opposite St Christophers Green and is now the fairground car park. Just east of this pit were the brickworks where around 1900 this horse-powered pug mill was used to puddle the clay before it was used to make bricks and tiles. The back of the Weaving House in Kings Road is immediately behind the horse. After John Grover bought the brickworks he re-located brick making to Hammer where there was a more plentiful supply of clay. He built Electra House (now Clay Hill House) in 1911 just to the east of the old disused clay pit. The Royal Haslemere Laundry, a building now replaced by the wine warehouse, was built on the site of the pug mill.

Since 1906 the fun fair has been held in May and September at the fairground car park. Around 1910 the traditional sideshows and rides were pulled to the fair by horses. But steam power was also used and even in the 1940s the author remembers being taken by his father to see two large showmans' engines parked near where the Wey Centre now stands. The bright electric light these were generating on that dark evening left a lasting impression on a young boy!

Development around Wey Hill began soon after 1900. The large shop and houses on the corner, then occupied by John Humphrey, a draper and furniture dealer, has been the public library since November 1947. Between 1939 and 1945 it was used as billets for soldiers. The track alongside this building led to the railway line where J. McLennon was the level crossing keeper in 1900; the present footbridge was built soon after. The road from the top of Wey Hill to the crossing had been known as Sicklemill Road but was re-named St Christopher's Road after the church was built. There was a sweet shop in the solitary building at the top of the hill but this was knocked down when the Haslemere & District Co-operative Society Stores were extended by the addition of a furniture department before the Second World War.

The Drill Hall at the eastern end of St Christopher's Green was built around 1908 by Sir Harry Waechter, who lived at Ramsters, near Chiddingfold. It was designed for training Territorial troops in one large hall which has since been sub-divided to provide office space for commercial use. The parade of Comrades of the Great War leaving the Drill Hall was probably part of the 1919 Peace Celebrations. The old drill hall was demolished in 2005.

Alfred and Lily Glover opened their first shop at 73 Wey Hill in 1929, a business that was to continue through three generations before the door closed in 2000 for the last time. In March 1938 this very full window display included wireless sets by Philips, McMichael, Lissen and HMV priced from 14s 6d to 10½ guineas as well as piano accordions and a banjo. The side window contained bicycle accessories, fishing tackle and gramophone records (78rpm) by Rex and Regent at 1s 6d each.

Across the road other Glover showrooms contained fine displays of bicycles and prams. Makes on show at 68 Wey Hill included Hercules, Humber, BSA and Rayleigh bicycles from £4 7s 6d to £7 17s 6d, Qualcast lawnmowers from £1 6s 6d and a Tamsad folding pram for only £1 9s 6d. All the bicycles were available on special weekly terms. Later Glover's opened their Babyland Department when Mrs Marshal's fried fish restaurant closed at 62 Wey Hill, just across the road from their original shop. During the 1950s, '60s and '70s Alfie Glover's widely-read and amusing 'Plum Pie' advertising column in the *Haslemere Herald* contained up-to-date offers introduced by his own news and views on life in Haslemere and the wider world.

The Regal Cinema first opened in October 1914 but closed in 1936, soon after the Rex Cinema opened at Shottermill. By May 1961 the prominent white building, where audiences had been thrilled by the latest movies, was being used by Farnham Lane Garage as a showroom for Vauxhall cars. Alfred Glover's shops were on either side of the road in the foreground. The small single-gabled building immediately beyond the old cinema was Kinema Cottage. Both buildings were demolished in the early 1960s and the site re-developed to provide Haslemere with its first small supermarket.

Miss Violet Kevan outside her shop at 74 Wey Hill in 1936. She had opened the library a year earlier and sold a variety of gifts, stationery and toys as well as providing a 'pay as you borrow' library for people living around Wey Hill and Shottermill. Similar libraries existed in the town at the Green Frog Bookshop in Petworth Road and at Boots the Chemist in the High Street. During the 1960s this shop became a greengrocers, The Fruitbowl, that closed in 1988 and is now a café.

An unseasonable fall of snow on 25 April 1908 had not stopped the milkman delivering to Oakleigh, the large house on the left built by George Rapson, the Lion Green blacksmith, around 1900. Next door was the premises of Messrs Arnold and Irish (see below) who occupied the building with advertising signs on the side wall and which has since been replaced by the Shottermill Branch of Lloyds Bank now an accountancy office. Soon after this photograph was taken work must have started on John Irish's new grocery shop which was built at the corner of St Christopher's Road and opened on 1 January 1909. Further along towards Lion Green the shop front of Arthur J. Bartlett, an undertaker and furniture remover, is just visible.

Brothers-in-law Keeble Arnold and John Irish shared this butchery and grocery shop in the early 1900s. John Irish had given up hopes of a career as a veterinary surgeon after his father was killed while playing cricket (see opposite). He soon met his future wife, Florence, who lived next door to the shop with her parents at Oakleigh. During the past forty years the house to the right has been used as a photographer's shop by Peter Waller, as officers for Lloyds Bank and most recently for the sale of office equipment and supplies.

John William Irish came to Haslemere from Hinton St George in Somerset following a tragic accident in which his father was killed by a cricket ball. In 1906 he married Florence Amelia Rapson, only daughter of George 'Curly' Rapson who was the blacksmith at Lion Green; the Methodist church was built on the site of his forge. This wedding group of the author's grandparents at Whitcombe, St Christophers Road, includes, from left to right: Keeble Arnold (see opposite) and his wife Jane who was John Irish's sister, John William Irish, Florence Amelia Irish and Walter Rapson who was one of Florence's six brothers.

A busy morning outside The Fruitbowl in 1973 with customers looking at the display of fruit and vegetables in front of the shop. Across the road Irish's grocery shop and attached house at 93 Wey Hill was about to be sold at auction as a re-development site. Next door are some of the new shops and flats built in the mid-1960s after Oakleigh was demolished.

A small school for children from five to eight years old was run by Miss Zillah Ford (back left) with Miss Lillian Welland (back right) at Upton Cott, St Christopher's Road. Pupils in 1921 included, left to right, back row: Irene Bridger, ? Smith, Irene Robinson, Ruby Irish, -?-, -?-, -?-. Middle row: Betty Buckett, -?-, -?-, Cyril Queen, Donald Stroud, Haswell Lambden. Front row: Peter Madgwick, Sylvia Oliver, Constance Cheeseman, -?-, Ruth Bromley, -?-, Norman Papps, ? Papps. The photograph was taken by Rupert Robinson who had his studio at 69 Wey Hill. Miss Ford later moved her school into Meadow Vale. Miss Welland opened Hillside School at her home, The Old House, on the corner of the High Street. The classrooms were at 2 Petworth Road from where a view of the stables at the back of the old Red Lion proved a great distraction from lessons when the farrier was at work – and often led to a severe reprimand as the author well remembers!

King George VI and Queen Elizabeth were crowned on 12 May 1937, an event which pharmacist Percy Bargery marked with a patriotic display in the window of his shop, next door to Miss Kevan's Library. This picture of the decorations was probably taken by Mr Bargery himself who was a keen amateur photographer.

Preston Huggins employed a number of local boys in the 1920s to deliver newspapers from his shop at the bottom of Wey Hill. Every summer they were rewarded by a trip to the seaside in a charabanc. This group waiting outside the shop for their transport to arrive included, from left to right: Johnny Frogley, ? Lambdin, ? Lambdin, Ron Heather, -?-, -?-, Sid Madgwick, Jack Pickaver, ? Walder, -?-, -?-, Preston Huggins. In the shop doorway are Nancy White and Kathleen Sadler with Margaret Waters to the right of Mr Huggins. To the left of the shop are the meadows where the first houses in Weysprings were built in 1940. The newspaper headline to the right reads 'Railways Grave Position' – not a lot has changed in the last eighty years!

This procession was part of the local Peace Celebrations in 1919 that took place in the High Street and on Lion Green. The banner was being carried by the Comrades of the Great War. On the corner Lion Green Stores was then owned by Charles Burgess who had another shop in Haslemere, the Broadway Stores on the corner of the High Street and West Street.

Looking across what is now a busy junction with traffic signals it is difficult to believe how peaceful this same spot was ninety years ago. The Red Lion public house was then kept by Henry Moorey. Next door, just right of the lamp-post, a house called Lynton was home to the Chuter family whose carriage-building works were in the sheds to the left. This house was later divided into two cottages which were demolished when the Co-operative supermarket was built in 1980. Just visible on the skyline, to the left of the street lamp, is the upper part of Weysprings House (see p. 100).

The 1919 Peace Celebrations on Lion Green just after the procession had arrived from Wey Hill. In the background the central group of buildings were the premises of J.S. Spring & Co. Ltd, having been used previously by Harry Booker in the 1880s and '90s, and then by John Chuter & Son from 1899, all of whom were carriage builders. Later this area was used as a coalyard by the Haslemere Co-operative Society. Behind the sheds are the wet meadows where Weysprings, a Rhodes development of individual houses so typical of mid-twentieth-century Haslemere, was built in 1940 and in the late 1950s.

Lion Lane showing how narrow the road was where it passed White Gable, the home of Mrs Stevens, c. 1910. By this time there had already been many new houses built further up the lane but it was not until the 1950s, when car ownership was becoming more the norm, that the roadway was widened. This unfortunately necessitated the demolition of the cottage behind the yew tree on the right.

St Christopher's Church, designed by architect Charles Spooner in the Arts & Crafts style, was built from local Bargate stone on the corner of Bunch Lane. It was needed for the overflow congregation from St Bartholomew's church who had to attend services at the New Educational Hall in Kings Road. The Revd James Macnab Watson was the first minister in 1903 when the church was consecrated. During the late 1930s the Revd C.C. Tanner was priest-in-charge. At the outbreak of war he joined the Royal Navy as chaplain on HMS *Fiji*. His ship was bombed and he sadly lost his life while bravely saving others from drowning.

In 1878 when John Wornham Penfold built this house in Farnham Lane it was called Heatherbank. The name soon changed to Weysprings House and it became the home of the Revd J. Wallace who founded the Three Counties Nursing Association (see p. 105). After his wife died John Wallace left Haslemere and the house was home for the next twenty years for Surgeon-General James Cleghorn and then his widow. After the Second World War Mr Tompkins of the Haslemere Cinema Company lived there. Today it is much altered and divided into two homes.

The high banks and sunken roadway of Farnham Lane around 1904 indicate an old route, deeply eroded in places by water and horse-drawn traffic. This was the old coach road from Hindhead to Chichester before the new turnpike road was built in the 1760s between Godalming and Haslemere. After travelling down this lane the coaches probably turned towards Sickle Mill, following the present-day route of St Christopher's Road to the railway line, then along the old hangar in Kings Road, above the new sports centre, before turning south past Sturt Farm to the Sussex border at Bell Vale. The driveway to the left in Farnham Lane was the original entrance to Weysprings House.

Twelve

Shottermill

The white weather-boarded buildings of Sickle Mill as they appeared across the mill pond in the middle of the nineteenth century. Since the eighteenth century the mill had been used by the Simmons family to manufacture paper. It was sold in 1854 to Messrs Appleton, a firm from London who manufactured braid for military uniforms. They were already using the mill at Elstead for this purpose and the purchase of Sickle Mill marked an expansion of their business which coincided with the Crimea War. It is not know why the very tall chimney was constructed at a water mill, who had it built, or when it was removed. During the latter part of the nineteenth century soldiers no longer went to war in bright and conspicuous uniforms. The resulting decline in the market for braid meant that Messrs Appleton no longer required Sickle Mill. It was sold by auction in 1911 and then acquired by Haslemere Urban District Council in the 1920s. The Herons Leisure Centre was built on the site of the mill pond in 1998.

Lane End Farm stood at Junction Place, by the original entrance to the Holy Cross Sanatorium. The track in front of the farmhouse is now Hindhead Road. Still a farm around 1880 it had become the Lodge to Shottermill Hall, owned by Miss Foster, at the turn of the century. Shottermill Hall later became home to the Congregation of the Daughters of the Cross. The Lodge, which was later rather heavily buttressed on the south side, must have been rather unstable and was demolished some time after the First World War.

Sturt Farm stands where there has been a farm for at least the last 700 years. The present farm is one of the last where dairy cattle have been kept close to the town during the last forty years. The house appears little changed since William Smithers farmed there in the early 1900s but the fine old barn behind burnt down some years ago. A sad note in the October 1906 issue of the *Haslemere Parish Magazine* extends sympathy to the Smithers family for the sad loss of their daughter Daisy after a painful and trying disease.

Looking across the fields in 1961 towards St Stephen's church. Dairy cows used to graze where now there are houses obscuring the view. On the left is the old army hut put up by Caleb Glover, who not only sold produce from his smallholding, but also dealt in both new and antique furniture. The hut also had many other uses including meetings of the Women's Institute, the Evangelical Church, as a Sunday school, for art classes and during the Second World War for furniture storage. It was dismantled in 1987 but only to continue a new life as a stable near Petersfield.

The choir at St Stephen's church in 1897 included, left to right, back row: R. Barkwill, W. Clapshaw, A. Harden, C. Covington (who was a draper and later postmaster at Lion Green), F. Tickner, Harry Rogers (who had a garage at Wey Hill), Alfred Rapson (son of George Rapson who was the blacksmith at Lion Green and also Parish Clerk), A. Chuter, F. Baker. Middle row: G. Harding, ? Bartlett, ? Archer, J. Barkwell, M. Marsh (who was the organist), Revd G.H. Purdue, Revd John Wallace (founder of the Three Counties Nursing Association (see pages 100 & 105)). ? Waller and ? Young are two of the four boys to the right of the Revd Wallace. Front row: S. Puttick, J. Harding, A. Harden, G. Barkwill, N. Hill, W. Moorey.

High above the road opposite the railway bridge at Shottermill was the Staff of Life public house. Publicans here at the turn of the last century included Thomas Snelling (1882), Charles Wase (1890), Mrs Jas Garland (1899), Edward John Stagg (1905-24) and Charles Lucas in 1927. The picture dates from the late 1920s with Johnny Rowe and Peggy Lucas outside – perhaps she was the daughter of Charles Lucas.

Mary Ann Evans, better known as George Eliot, wrote *Middlemarch* while living at Brookbank in the early 1870s, a house just above the Staff of Life and next door to the old Shottermill post office. Visitors to the house during her stay included Alfred Lord Tennyson and the artist Helen Allingham, who painted watercolours of nearby scenes including Rose Cottage. Later Brookbank, which had been described by Thomas Wright as a 'queer cottage', was divided into two with the part nearer the railway keeping the original name while the other half became known as Middlemarch.

The public elementary school at Shottermill was built in 1892, together with an attached house for the headmaster, on land between the Hindhead and Liphook Roads. It was enlarged in 1896 and by the early 1900s had places for 154 pupils; the infants went to a separate school in Church Road. In about 1927 a new school was built in Lion Lane and the old school building was used as a confectionery warehouse. It is now part of Shottermill Club, expanded from the original Workmen's Club which had been built at a cost of over £300 in 1892 on land given by James Simmons whose family had been paper makers at Sickle Mill.

The Three Counties Nursing Association was founded in 1897 by the Revd John Wallace, a retired missionary who had come to live at Weysprings House. The Association nurses provided home medical help for poorer people in the community. They lived in a Nurses' Home at Shottermill. The first home was situated between the school and the churchyard. In 1906 a new home was built to provide dormitory accommodation for the staff. This later became a private house, Nuthatches, which was demolished when Shottermill House was built on the corner opposite St Stephen's church.

The Holy Cross Hospital was developed around Shottermill Hall (centre, right) from 1917 as a sanatorium to treat people suffering from tuberculosis. Treatment required plenty of fresh air and the block to the left had open-fronted wards on two floors. Later, as the treatment of TB changed following the discovery of antibiotics, these wards were enclosed. During the past few years the whole complex has been extensively changed and much new housing built in the grounds around the hospital.

Lunchtime in the dining room at the Holy Cross sanatorium sometime during the 1930s.

106

After St Stephen's church was built in 1841 the parish of Shottermill was unable at first to provide accommodation for a vicar and the post was filled temporarily by the Revd Candy who lived at The Lodge in Haslemere High Street. It was not until 1851 that a fine stone vicarage was built at Junction Place. Later, when this was replaced by a new vicarage, the old vicarage became the home of Miss Croft before becoming Jefferys Garage in the 1930s. Later Stephencroft Motors used the house as offices until it was knocked down in 1996 and the whole site redeveloped as a modern filling station.

Shottermill Women's Institute Players performing *Cranford* on 28 March 1930 at a Hambledon group meeting. From left to right the players were Miss Clark, Mrs Rees, Mrs Huscombe, Miss Groves, -?-, Mrs Rossie (sic), Mrs Whiterod, -?-, Mrs Dunnings.

Frensham Hall stands on the north side of Woolmer Hill, facing east across the Nutcombe Valley to Frensham Hall Farm below. Before the Second World War it was home to Joan, Countess of Cawdor who employed a number of local people in service, some of whom were able to travel to Scotland with her when she stayed at the family home in Nairnshire. Later Frensham Hall became a nunnery but it is now a private house once again.

The road to Hindhead in the 1920s was very narrow at the point where it passed the entrance to Frensham Hall Farm. In the 1930s Haslemere Urban District Council cut the bank on the right back to its present position. Previously this road had been maintained by Hambledon Rural District Council (see p. 63).

Pitfold Mill stood on the east-side of Critchmore Lane, almost opposite Pitfold Farm. During the nineteenth century it had belonged to James Simmons but was being used for dressing leather by Edwin Masters in 1882 and by Messrs Gent & Davies between 1887 and 1899. During much of the twentieth century chestnut fencing was made here by several different makers, the last being Jimmy Homewood. The buildings were later demolished and the mill site is now part of the housing estate on the corner opposite Border Road.

New Mill stood just to the south of Pitfold Mill, through the narrow bridge under the railway line. It was also owned by James Simmons as part of his paper-making business (see p. 101). From the mid-1880s Messrs Gent & Davies, who were leather dressers at Pitfold Mill, probably also used New Mill. By the end of the First World War rabbits were being bred in the dilapidated old buildings. The mill pond disappeared during the 1930s and the mill was demolished in 1976.

Critchmere Manor House as it appeared in about 1930. This fine building, also known as Pitfold Farm, was demolished about forty years ago and replaced by houses. The name is still remembered as Manor Close, the small development of bungalows built on the sire of the old house.

The Royal Oak at Critchmere was photographed by John Wornham Penfold in October 1876, some time before the present frontage was added. In most late nineteenth and early twentieth century trade directories it is referred to as a beer house. The wall in the left foreground crosses what is now the junction of Critchmere Lane and Woolmer Hill.

Thirteen
Sport and Entertainment

The Haslemere Hall was a most generous gift to the people of the town by Lewis Barclay Day although, sadly, he died before it was completed in 1914 to a design by local architect Annesley Brownrigg. During the First World War it was used as a soldiers' club. Since that time, and thanks to the efforts of a dedicated group of volunteers, it has provided a venue for many great moments of entertainment with plays, concerts, dances, meetings and, since the demise of the Rex Cinema, films. The annexe, built in 1963, now partly obscures this view of the hall.

HASLEMERE FESTIVAL
OF CHAMBER MUSIC

UNDER THE DIRECTION OF

Photo by Alvcyn L. Coburn.

ARNOLD DOLMETSCH
July 17th to July 29th, 1933.

The now world-famous Dolmetsch Festival of Chamber Music was begun by Arnold Dolmetech in 1925. This leaflet advertised the twelve concerts in the Ninth Festival. Prices for reserved seats ranged from £1 15s 0d to £3 10s 0d for the series of concerts and from 3s 6d to 8s 6d for a single concert. The agent for tickets was Messrs Charman in the High Street (now Nobbs) where a full programme was also available for a shilling.

In the days before the Haslemere Hall had been built many plays and concerts were performed on the stage in Haslemere School. The Haslemere Players first production of *The Pirates of Penzance* took place in 1911 and the cast are pictured outside the school. They included Lawford Benson (Frederic), Dorothy Bromley (Ruth), Hilda Brownrigg (Edith), Alan Chandler (Sergeant of Police), Katherine Chandler (Isabel), D. Fitzmaurice (Samuel), A.L. Gaskin (Pirate King), A.N. Lucey (Major General) and Janet Oram from D'Oyly Carte (Mabel). The musical director was W.E. Muir.

Haslemere Cricket Club had a reasonable season in 1904 when they won twelve of the twenty-three matches they played with four matches drawn and seven lost. The players were from left to right, back row: Farminer (umpire), Brisley, -?-, Madgwick, King (behind), F. Madgwick, L. Bromley, Parbury, Saunders (scorer). Middle row: Revd R.F. Carlisle, M. Madgwick, R.J. Hutchinson, A.L. Gaskin. Front row: Brown, C. Brisley. The photograph was probably taken at the old cricket ground in Church Lane, where the hospital and health centre were built later in the century.

The Haslemere Workmens' or Constitutional Club for the use of local men was built in 1886 by James Stewart Hodgson next door to the Swan Inn. The club was later bought by Mr & Mrs William Muir and presented to the Haslemere Branch of the Comrades of the Great War in November 1919. The group playing billiards around 1910 includes a master from Haslemere School (extreme right, and see p. 26) who, during the First World War at another Surrey school in Betchworth, organised the pupils to collect blackberries and awarded a prize for the class with the largest harvest.

Haslemere Football Club were winners of the Surrey Junior League Division 1 in the 1908-09 season. The team and club officials were, left to right, back row: Revd A.M. Watson (Joint Hon. Sec.), A.E. Prevett, J. Madgwick (referee). Middle row: G.H. Dean (Joint Hon. Sec.), P. Moorey, J. Stevens, C. Nightingale (Sub-captain), G. Hellier, S.A. Smith, E. Lewis (Linesman). Front row: C.H. Arthurs, R.M. Burman, F. Bargery, F. Madgwick (Captain, also see the cricket team on p. 113), G. Stallard.

Haslemere Boy Scouts in 1912. Left to right, back row: J. Lamboll, W. Maides, J. Weekes, W. Phillips, F. Bartlett, J. Madgwick, L. Moorey, J. Tyrrell, F. Weeks. Middle row: Assistant Scoutmaster Robertson, Scoutmaster F.C. Madgwick, Assistant Scoutmaster Mills. Front row: G. Moorey, C. Jones, L. Moorey, R. Phillips, L. Bartlett, C. Bowden.

The Rex Cinema was built for the Haslemere Cinema Co. Ltd opposite Shottermill Club by Chapman, Lowry & Puttick and opened in 1936. The manager was Mr Tomkins until 1953 when Richard Killinger took over the day-to-day running of the cinema. It closed in 1986 and was demolished soon after to be replaced by a block of flats.

On 22 September 1942 a British night stalker aeroplane, a type used to find German bombers with its nose-mounted searchlight, crashed between the Holy Cross Hospital and the Rex. Parts of the aeroplane, a Havoc Mark III attached to 1455 Flight, fell into the auditorium of the cinema during a matinée performance. Only one person in the audience was hurt seriously but the Havoc's crew of three, Flying Officer W.M.W. Winter, Pilot Officer J.H. Lindley and Flight Sergeant W.E.N. Cleall were, sadly, killed. Mrs Harman organised a collection from local shops and a donation was sent to their Commanding Officer in Lincolnshire.

Beacon Hill School Football Team in 1932 was trained by the headmaster, Gerald Echlin (right). The team included, left to right, back row: Vic Voller (Linesman), Tom Bumpstead, George Wren (Goalkeeper), Cecil Mullard, Roger Barnes. Middle row: Bob Glasher, Arthur Woods, Doug Ellis (Captain, with the ball), Alan Punter, Chris Court. Sitting on the ground were Kenneth Warr and Bob Mullard. The 1932 season had been successful for the team although George Wren did not recall beating their nearest neighbours from Churt that year.

This team from Hindhead Cricket Club had a very successful season in 1948 when they were winners of the British Legion (Surrey County) Cup. They were, left to right, back row: W.T. Peskett (Hon. Treasurer), F. Rowberry (Vice-captain), H.G. Snelling (Hon. Secretary). Middle row: W. Stevens, C. Prior, J.S.A. Mattock, P. Mulliner, C. Higdon. Front row: L. Heather, P. Huntingford, C. Pratt (Captain), F.N. da Costa, Esq. (President), A. Wheeler, J. Dopson, C. Hill.

Fourteen

Bramshott Chase
and the Canadians

A public house called the Seven Thorns, named originally after the trees which grew on the opposite side of the London to Portsmouth Road, has stood at Bramshott Chase for about 500 years. This 1878 view was recorded by John Wornham Penfold while his groom waited patiently with the carriage outside the entrance to the inn. At this time trade was probably at a very low ebb since the London to Portsmouth coaches had been superseded by the train service from Waterloo and regular motor traffic was still some twenty-five to thirty years in the future. The delivery cart belonged to James Louch who had a shop in Bramshott where he was also the sub-postmaster.

About fifty years after Mr Penfold took his photograph (see previous page) the fortunes of the Seven Thorns had been revived by visitors in motor cars and charabancs from far and wide – the car outside the hotel, as it was now known, was registered in Kent. The front of the building had been altered by this time with the addition of two porches, the roof line had been changed and an extension built at the right hand end. Proprietors between the two world wars included George Leslie Baillie-Hamilton and Ayton & Wilkinson.

This advertising postcard, which dates from the same time as the picture above, shows the dining room of the Seven Thorns set for a formal lunch or dinner, perhaps a wedding celebration, with a waiter and waitress ready to attend to the diners' every need. How things have changed as the future of the now ruined building, known latterly as the Spaniards, is debated by planners – will houses eventually replace the old coaching inn?

Gorselands Hotel, seen here in the 1920s, had been a private house until it was used as the Divisional Headquarters for the Canadian Expeditionary Forces who were based at Bramshott Camp from 1916 to 1919. When the army left it became an hotel whose proprietors included Ernest Molyneux in 1923 and Mr and Mrs Herbert Harris during the 1930s, when the cost of a room was from 2½ guineas per week. The building was used for a while as a Little Chef and later a café. It is now set back from the new A3 approach road to the Hindhead Tunnel, due to open by the summer of 2011.

The hospital at Bramshott Camp was built by the British Army on the south side of the present A3 road, just on the Liphook side of the Seven Thorns. The hospital opened on 15 November 1915 but soon became part of the large Canadian Infantry Base Camp that was on Bramshott Common from 1916 to 1919. According to the message on this postcard, sent in April 1918, the first four huts on the left were wards while the one beyond housed administrative offices and the laboratory. The hut behind the tents was the chest annexe. At the end of the war, in 1918, an influenza epidemic caused the deaths of many soldiers who were waiting to return home to Canada. There was also a Candian Army Hospital on Bramshott Common during the Second World War.

Several recreation huts were provided by different organizations at Bramshott Camp. This one was known as the Camp Home and was run by the Soldiers' Christian Association. All soldiers were welcome to use the reading, writing and recreation room where rows of tables and chairs were available, giving people the opportunity to relax a little and write letters home to families far away in Canada.

A group of soldiers from various regiments, many wearing kilts, together with local people who helped to provide some comforts for men so far from home. This group is outside another Soldiers' Christian Association hut. In a camp as large as Bramshott there would have been other recreation huts provided by groups such as the YMCA and NACB (Navy and Army Canteen Board). The latter organization also ran the Gaiety Theatre in the camp. This was later also used as a cinema where local people, as well the military personnel, were able to see some of the latest silent movies before the war ended and the whole camp site was cleared of buildings.

On the north side of the London to Portsmouth road a small 'Tin Town' of shops was operated by local people. Mrs Jack Edwards (centre) from Fernhurst opened a shop and café which sold all sorts of food, sweets and large quantities of pencils to write letters home. It seems to have been very popular with patients from the hospital across the road who had recovered enough to visit her premises. Dolly West (right of the till) was one of the local girls who helped in the shop.

A few of the many thousands of Canadian soldiers who saw Bramshott Camp as a temporary base while on their way to France and Belgium. The author's grandparents lived at Liphook Station where their son, as a young boy, took jugs of cool lemonade, home-made by his mother, to give to men confined to hot railway carriages on their way to the front lines. Often he was given cap badges or shoulder tags in return; unfortunately these were all thrown away in the 1920s.

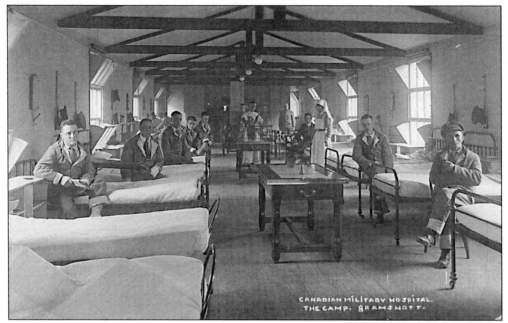

Conditions in the wards at the camp hospital were rather basic; there were few of the home comforts far away in Canada for these men recovering from wounds received, or illnesses caught, while in a foreign land. Note, however, that the ward is lit by electric light, an advantage not shared by the recreation huts where oil lamps were used.

During the First World War several large houses in the area were used as military hospitals. This group of soldiers in the distinctive pale blue uniforms they wore while convalescing, together with some nurses and the padre, had moved from Bramshott Camp to High Rough Convalescent Home at the top of Farnham Lane in Haslemere.

Fifteen

Grayshott

Crossways Road, seen here in 1910, was the nucleus around which Grayshott had developed during the previous fifteen to twenty years. On the left is Victoria Terrace where Madame Warr and Company sold drapery and millinery in several of the small shops. Opposite is Jubilee Terrace, presumably so-called because both this and Victoria Terrace had been built at about the time of Queen Victoria's Diamond Jubilee in 1897. Mr Munday had a green grocery shop at the centre of the terrace and there was a bicycle shop to the right, next door to the post office which was behind the telephone post. It was there that Flora Thompson was assistant to the postmaster Walter Chapman. Later, the post office moved to a shop nearer the church, where it still is today. At Edinburgh House, on the extreme right, Miss Marion Menzies sold china as well as providing teas and accommodation for visitors to the village.

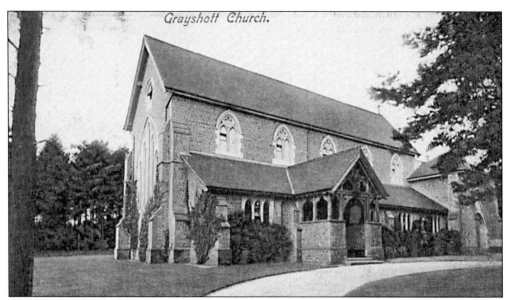

Grayshott Church.

Grayshott was part of the parish of Headley but, as the village developed and the population grew, the need for a separate church became apparent. St Luke's church was built on land given by Miss C.B. I'Anson and the foundation stone was laid by her on 3 September 1898. The building was completed just over a year later and first used on 17 October 1899. It was consecrated on St Luke's Day, 18 October 1900. The tower and spire had been included in the original design by Edward I'Anson but were not built until 1910.

Fox and Pelican Hotel, Grayshott.

The Fox and Pelican was built by the local firm, Messrs Chapman and Puttick, for the People's Refreshment House Association at a cost of £1,465 plus furnishings. The name was chosen because the emblem of Bishop Fox of Winchester, a founder of the association, was a pelican. The original sign, shown in the inset, was painted by Walter Crane, the great Victorian illustrator.

Crossways Road in the mid-1950s with plenty of room to park! On the left Dale White sold china and glass in what had been called Edinburgh House while next door was Gould and Chapman's furniture shop. Across the road was Will Wright's bicycle shop where you could have your old machine repaired or buy a new one.

Frederick Harris and his employees outside the shop in Crossways Road from where in the 1920s bicycles and motorcycles of many different makes could be purchased. Some of the great names in evidence on the windows include BSA, Raleigh and Royal Enfield. Petrol was sold from a pump to the left of the shop. Mr Harris also had a second shop in Liphook.

Grayshott Village Hall was built 100 years ago and opened on 23 May 1902. It can seat up to 300 people but, at the time, seemed rather large perhaps since the population then was little more than twice that number. However, demand for such a facility was so great that a second, but smaller, hall was also built. Both halls are now run by a Management Committee which includes some members of the Parish Council. This postcard view was sent by Ern(est) Tickner to Godalming in December 1914.

The Massacres
IN
MACEDONIA.

A
PUBLIC & NON-POLITICAL
MEETING
WILL BE HELD IN
THE VILLAGE HALL, GRAYSHOTT,
ON
Saturday, Sept. 26, 1903,
At 8 p.m.,
To consider the Terrible Events
now happening in Macedonia.

S. MARSHALL BULLEY, ESQ.
In the Chair.

The following, among many others, hope to be present :—

Sir A. Conan Doyle, D.L., Hon. Rollo Russell,
Dr. Lyndon, Miss James, Revs. G. B. Stallworthy
and A. Kluht, Dr. Gilbert Smith,
A. Ingham Whitaker, Esq., Aneurin Williams, Esq.
&c., &c.

CRADDOCK, PRINTER, GODALMING.

A flyer advertising one of the first meetings held in the village hall. Almost a century later it seems that very little has changed in some parts of the world.

During the Edwardian period Grayshott also developed quickly along the Headley Road so that by 1915 there were many small shops stretching from the village hall to the junction with Crossways Road. But even by this time there was little evidence of motor vehicles. However, the state of the road shows that it was used frequently by horses and a large hay cart is just visible outside the White Heather Dairy in the distance.

Walter Winchester of Glen Road used this ex-War Department Daimler lorry to deliver coal during the 1920s. House coal and anthracite were the usual fuels at this time when Walter and his lorry kept the scuttles of Grayshott and Hindhead full and the home fires burning.

The Zachary Merton Convalescent Home stood at the eastern end of Kingswood Firs with the entrance, top left, coming in from Crossways Road, quite close to the junction with the Portsmouth Road. This home, and another in Surrey, were built by the Baroness de Hirsch Foundation to give Jewish people suffering from tuberculosis a chance of fresh air in the country away from London. The funding for this foundation originated from Maurice, Baron de Hirsch (1831-96), a member of a Bavarian banking family who had made a large, personal fortune through the construction of the Balkans railways under concession from the Ottoman Government. There was also a school at the home. Some local children attended classes here in the 1950s when the school in Grayshott did not have room for all the pupils.

This group of members from the Victory Lodge of the Royal and Ancient Order of the Buffalo, Grayshott were waiting to depart on a summer outing, c. 1920. The bus, a Daimler, belonging to the Aldershot & District Traction Company, is probably from the garage at Wey Hill. I do hope you have all found this journey around the Haslemere area as enjoyable as we hope the group above did on their outing some ninety years ago.

128